Jesus

plus

nothing

Jesus

plus

nothing

tim timmons

EMBERS PRESS

EMBERS PRESS

2618 San Miguel
Box #221
Newport Beach, CA 92660
www.embersfellowship.com

© 2012 Tim Timmons

ISBN: 978-0-9842429-2-4

Unless otherwise indictated, Scripture quotations are taken from the *Holy Bible, Today's New International Version* (TNIV). Copyright © 2001, 2005 by Biblica®. Used by permission. All rights reserved.

Scripture quotations marked The Message are taken from *The Message,* copyright © by Eugene H. Peterson, 1993, 1994, 1995, 1996, 2000, 2001, 2002. Used by permission of NavPress Publishing Group.

Printed in the United States

I am afraid that, as the serpent deceived Eve by his craftiness, your minds will be led astray from the simplicity and purity of devotion to Christ.

Paul

2 Corinthians 11:3

CONTENTS

INTRODUCTION 1

Part I – missing the point

Chapter 1–   Is Jesus Plus Nothing Enough? 19

Chapter 2–   Are "Liar, Lunatic, Lord" Our Only Options? 29

Chapter 3–   What Were My Blinders? 45

Chapter 4–   What Was Israel's Blinkered Thinking? 59

Chapter 5–   How Does Jesus Plus Nothing
Become Everything But Jesus? 79

Chapter 6–   How Can You Expect to Reach the
World for God without God
First Reaching Your Heart? 93

Part II – the pre-eminence of Jesus

Chapter 7–   Was Jesus a Christian? 103

Chapter 8–   Does Jesus Trump Everything? 113

Part III – the presence of the kingdom

Chapter 9–   Did Jesus Launch a Church or a
Movement? 135

Chapter 10–   What Are the Secrets Jesus Revealed
about the Kingdom? 153

Part IV – the power of the few

Chapter 11–   Was the Cross the Finished
Work of Jesus? 169

Chapter 12–   When Does Jesus Show Up

and What Happens When He Does? 181

Part V – simply following Jesus plus nothing

Chapter 13–   What Is the Jesus Manifesto? 193

Chapter 14–   What Does It Mean to

Be a Follower of Jesus? 207

Chapter 15–   What Are the Three Vital

Habits in Following Jesus? 217

Chapter 16–   What Does It Look

Like to Show Off Jesus? 227

Chapter 17–   What Is Your End Game? 235

CONCLUSION 247

Hi, I'm Tim Timmons.
And I'm an addict.

Once you've pulled yourself off the floor, I want to ask you something. What was the first thought that came to mind when you heard those words?

Tim Timmons? One-time D.T.S. prof? Former pastor of a mega-church before anyone knew what a mega-church was? Popular speaker? Bestselling author? That Tim Timmons?
He's an addict?
Who knew?

The way I should have introduced myself is:
I'm Tim Timmons.
And I *was* an addict.

Oh, good, you may be thinking. *He's over it. He's been to rehab, he's clean and sober, the prodigal has come home and he's back in the saddle, doing ministry.*

If you thought that, you would be wrong. Let me explain. In my years of counseling, a lot of people have come into my office, seeking help for their addictions. The addiction could be drugs, sex, alcohol, food, spending, gambling. What brought them to my office was that the addiction was ruining their lives. It was ruining their health, their marriage, their relationships, their work, their spiritual life. By the time they came to me, they were desperate. The life they were living was killing them—along with everything dear to them—and that is why they came.

They wanted help. They wanted to be healthy, to be whole, to be healed of whatever it was that drove them to whatever pain-killers they were now dependent on.

The first step to getting healthy is to admit you *need* help. And you do that by admitting you are an addict.

Of all the addictions, none is as insidious as religion. *Religion?*

You don't have to whisper it. Yes, religion. It is the closet addiction no one talks about. Here is what I have learned after spending almost my entire career in that closet. No drug is so addictive. None offers such a high. And none is so hard to break.

Compounding the problem, it's legal. No one is going to take away your keys to the Kingdom if you're a religion addict. No one is going to stage an intervention. No one is going to tell you to cut back, to get help, to give it up. Just the opposite. You are going to be everyone's go-to guy or go-to girl when something needs to be done in your church or organization. You're going to be the one they ask to head the committee. You're going to be the one they want on point, because you're the person who can get it done and get it done right.

Let's face it, something about that *is* intoxicating. It feels good to be needed. To be wanted. To be thought of like that. Depended upon like that. It makes shots at the bar seem like light beer by comparison.

Here's the thing about the highs of addiction. They don't last. Don't get me wrong. Those first couple of drinks *are* relaxing. That rush from the prescription drug *does* take the edge off your pain. And bringing home that new dress, those new shoes, that new purse, those cute little earrings—let's be honest, it *does* make you feel better, doesn't it?

But after the high, there's the hangover. Or the withdrawal. Or the sobering reality when the credit card bill comes at the end of the month. And so, to get over that pain, we go shopping again . . . to the medicine cabinet again . . . to the liquor cabinet again, if you're too ashamed to drink in public, or to the bar again, if you're too afraid to drink alone.

Let me be clear. If you think I am talking about just another drug dependency issue, alcoholism, or some other addiction, I am not. I am talking about addiction to religion, which was my addiction and maybe is yours. I'm talking about more than that, though. I'm talking about a whole culture that has been in the throes of addiction for so long it thinks the drunken state is the normal state. It thinks staggering is the way *everyone* walks; slurred speech, the way *everyone* talks; hung-over, the way *everyone* feels in the morning.

Our Christian culture has been on a bender so long it can't see itself the way other people at the party see it. And it's not a pretty picture. Trust me, I've heard the hushed conversations while we're in the room, along with the harsh criticisms when we've left.

To be honest . . . after looking at my past self in the mirror . . . I think the revulsion is justified.

My History As a Christian

This is the story of my past, the story of how I got addicted to religion and how I got clean and sober. Like most addictions, mine started early . . .

As an only child, I was driven to perform. My parents expected me to be the best, and I did my best to live up to their expectations. I was the first on either side of the family to go to college. It was a Christian Liberal Arts college, where I was a favorite among my professors and a leader among my peers. After college I went to seminary. And not just any seminary, *Dallas Theological Seminary*, which was the best, according to those professors and those peers.

I performed well and when I graduated, I left that academic nest on the updrafts of everyone's highest hopes. By then, I had degrees, acclaim, an extensive library of books on fixing people, and a waiting list of people who needed to be fixed.

I put out my shingle: "Tim Timmons. Equipped for Ministry." And I started my practice. I had such a great start, or so it seemed to me then. The best theological training. A pot of riches in terms of gifting. And a passion to change the world, one person at a time, one book at a time, one crowd at a time.

I lacked only one thing.

Jesus.

At best, I used his statements in the Gospels as proof-texts to be used in evangelistic discussions and debates. But I didn't love him. At least, not the way he was loved by those who first knew him, first followed him.

What I loved was performing. And by now, I was good at it. It made my parents proud, my family proud, my college proud, my seminary proud. And that felt good. *Really* good.

But I craved more. One more exhilarating counseling appointment, where I turned someone's life around. One more dynamic speaking engagement, where I moved the crowd. One more bestseller, where I . . .

. . . could get high again.

I lost my parents by the time I was 26, before they could see much of my success. The loss was painful. My response to the pain?

Another round of more.

More counseling, more speaking, more writing.

But it wasn't enough. It was never enough. Why? Because the Jesus I knew wasn't enough. How could he be?

4

How could a Jesus who was largely unknown to me be enough to give life to me, and through me to give life to others? Oh, I knew a lot *about* him—just look at my library. But I didn't *know* him. Not the real Jesus, anyway.

In my youth I was introduced to a legalistic, judgmental Jesus, one with high expectations and a low tolerance for slackers. From time to time I had glimmers of the real Jesus—the Jesus who was full of love and grace and compassion—but those glimpses were few and fleeting. Most of the time he seemed far away. And frankly, I didn't have the time to find him, let alone to follow him.

Why?

Driven people don't *have* a lot of time. And I was not only driven, I was driven to be the best—to write the most popular books, to preach the most stirring sermons, to build the biggest church, create the best counseling centers, establish the most extensive network of hotlines to help people in crisis.

With respect to the church I started, from the first Sunday to the last we never experienced anything but growth. We set up 70 chairs for our first gathering, and more than 400 people showed up. The month of my resignation, 10 years later, we had more than 6,900 families participating in the many services and activities.

But it wasn't enough.

With respect to speaking, I was trained to speak on the largest platforms in the world—whether the audiences were religious or secular. Once on the speakers' circuit, I had one of the largest motivational platforms in the country, with audiences ranging from 5000 to 35,000, and with as many bookings as I wanted.

But it wasn't enough.

With respect to writing, publishers paid me significant advances just for signing a contract and handing them an outline. I had 10 bestsellers to my name, each of them advertised in Christian magazines, promoted on Christian radio, endorsed by a constellation of Christian stars, grateful letters coming in from all their readers, royalty checks rolling in every quarter.

But it wasn't enough.

Whenever my esteem was low and I needed another fix of affirmation, I went to the mall. I was sure to run into people who needed help or who had already been helped by me. Or I would visit the bookstores where I could see my books on display and be greeted enthusiastically by the sales' staff or the customers.

With respect to counseling, every hour was Happy Hour, at least for me. I loved it. I found that when I mixed my gifting and my training with my addiction, it was a pretty potent cocktail. Over the years, I have counseled thousands. The needs were longer than the day was long, and most evenings when I left the office, several people were in the parking lot around my car, wanting to see me about their problems. I have painful memories of driving away from those people who were hurting, unable to give them any kind of help other than to hug them and say, "Hang in there!"

Given the time, though, I felt I could "fix" almost anyone, no matter the problem. And that fueled my addiction. When my words or my compassion helped someone, it was the greatest drug ever. Like any addiction, though, once the euphoria wears off, you have to have more. I craved more, and I always found a way to get more. More situations where I could get my fix—counseling, speaking, parties, hospital visits, round the clock availability to everyone in every possible emergency.

As I look back on it, I had a Messiah complex. People were always in need, and I was always in need of being the one to meet their needs. Though exhausting, it was exhilarating.

But it wasn't enough.

With respect to teaching and preaching, I loved doing

that more than anything else. I was trained by the best to persuade an audience to action. It wasn't through an emotional show or by dazzling them with my footwork. I really did understand what it took to move an audience—the more hostile, the better. I was intoxicated with the heady powers of persuasion. If my primary addiction was fixing individuals, my secondary addiction was fixing the masses. Helping one person was a high, but helping thousands was the greatest high of all.

My teaching was a mixing-bowl blend of psychological principles, biblical texts, down-to-earth applications, with a good measure of Christianity thrown in. If Jesus was ever put into the mix, it was just a pinch, for flavor. In my mind, he was part of the message, but never central to the message. More and more, he got left behind. Don't get me wrong. Many were helped during that time. Some even found faith in God. But though they might have come to the conclusion that Jesus plus Tim Timmons was enough, they never got the impression that Jesus alone was enough.

With respect to my family, my addiction, my need for approval, affirmation—and dare I say it, applause—was killing them. Each of them suffered in their own way from my absence. After years of living like this, everything started to crumble. My marriage, my family, my passion. I was exhausted—physically, emotionally, and spiritually. I was frustrated, disillusioned, and I felt like a fraud.

How did I lose my way? I cried out from the throes of withdrawal.

And how—if ever—could I find my way to enough?

The History of Christianity

The history of Christianity is an ancient story, beset with its own addictions. Like most addictions, it started early . . .

For the first three hundred years of its existence, Christianity was a despised religion; and Christians, a persecuted minority. But then came Constantine, ruler of the Roman Empire, who allegedly saw a sign of the cross in the clouds, assuring him that by this sign he would conquer. In 315 A.D., Constantine signed an imperial edict, not only ending three centuries of state-sponsored persecution, but making Christianity the official state religion. The State had finally embraced the Church. And the Church had returned the embrace. At best, it was an unequally yoked union; at worst, an unholy union.

Almost immediately, pagan temples were destroyed, along with their priests. By 356 A.D., attending pagan services became punishable by death. By the fifth century, when the Christian emperor Theodosius reigned, he went so far as to have children executed for playing with fragments of pagan statues. By the sixth century, pagans were stripped of their rights, just as the Jews had been stripped of their rights in Nazi Germany.

But it wasn't enough.

During the eighth century, Charlemagne waged war against those whom the Roman Empire had determined were heathens. His battle cry was "Saxony must be Christianized, or wiped out." He proceeded to do just that. During his reign, most of Europe's indigenous cultures were obliterated. The height of atrocities took place in 782 A.D., when Charlemagne captured a hoard of Saxons in battle. He herded them to a river and there gave them the choice— be baptized in the name of the Lord Jesus Christ or be beheaded. More than four thousand lost their heads that day. By the year 800, Charlemagne was crowned Emperor of the Holy Roman Empire by Pope Leo III. In 1165, he was canonized as a saint. All of this for the ruthless and relentless war he waged, known as the Thirty Years' War.

But it wasn't enough.

History is written by the victors, not the vanquished, and that is why we don't hear much about the atrocities committed throughout Church history. The Crusades, for example. It's hard to find histories written by Jews during the Crusades, or by Muslims, or by the numerous Christian sects that refused the yoke of the Holy Roman Empire. Why? The witnesses were wiped out.

On the command of Pope Urban II in 1095, the Crusades began. Jerusalem was conquered on July 15, 1099, leaving more than 60,000 men, women, and children slaughtered in the streets. The Archbishop of Tyre, who witnessed the slaughter, wrote: "It was impossible to look upon the vast numbers of the slain without horror; everywhere lay fragments of human bodies, and the very ground was covered with the blood of the slain. It was not only the spectacle of headless bodies and mutilated limbs strewn in all directions that roused the horror of all who looked upon them. Still more dreadful was it to gaze upon the victors themselves, dripping with blood from head to foot, an ominous sight, which brought terror to all who met them. It is reported that within the Temple enclosure alone about ten thousand infidels perished."

Still, it wasn't enough.

The next month, the armies of the Holy Roman Empire marched to the coastal city of Ashkelon. More than 200,000 "heathens" were purged from the land, as one of the victors wrote, "in the name of Our Lord Jesus Christ."

Yet it wasn't enough.

On the Fourth Crusade, on April 12, 1204, Constantinople was captured, plundered, and sacked, the number of victims unknown. Figures vary, but by the end of the Crusades, Christians had killed between 20-60 million people.

Twenty to sixty million.

People.

Each made in the image of God. Each had a name. Each name had a story. And each story was cut short with a sword or a spear or some unspeakably gruesome means of torture.

9

The blood of Christian conquest stained the pages of history, seeping through the centuries and spreading across continents. Columbus, for example. You probably first read about him in elementary school, but certainly no later than middle school. You may remember the holiday named after him, but do you remember the history?

Here is some of his story, the part that got edited out of most textbooks. Columbus was a slave-trader by profession, setting sail across the Atlantic to seek new worlds. In his personal logbook he wrote why: "to bring the Gospel of Jesus Christ to the heathens." Though he found the people of the new world loving and generous, by the time of his second voyage, his men looted their villages, killed their animals, and slaughtered or else enslaved the villagers. Columbus' son, Fernando, chronicled the atrocities. If the natives resisted, Columbus countered their resistance by saying: "With the help of God . . . we shall make war against you in all ways and manners that we can, and shall subject you to the yoke of obedience to the Church and of Their Highness. We shall take you and your wives and your children, and shall make slaves of them."

But making slaves of them wasn't enough. On that second voyage Spanish soldiers invented all manner of gruesome ways to purge the land of these "infidels." They built low gallows, where the toes of those who hung on them barely touched the ground. The gallows had room for thirteen natives . . . in honor of Christ and his twelve disciples. And while they dangled there, the Spaniards wrapped straw around their bodies and burned them. By the end of the first decade after Columbus' discovery of the Caribbean Islands, the indigenous population dropped by a third in some places and by almost half in others. Before the end of the next century, those populations were all but wiped from the face of the earth.

I'm not exaggerating to make a point.

These things happened.

They happened "in the name of our Lord Jesus Christ."

And—God, help us—they are happening still.

We have beaten our swords into words and our spears into sound bites. With them we wage war. Instead of actual wars, they are cultural wars. We do this because we believe we have cornered the market on truth. Not only do we believe we have cornered the market; we believe we have the concession rights to that corner. The result has been the marketing of Christianity. And so the marketing mantra of the 21st century Church has become: "BIGGER, BETTER, FASTER!"

More. More. More.

As if "mega" wasn't enough.

The exclamation point at the end of the mantra is supposed to excite us about the voyage to the new world that awaits us, if only we can get onboard with the program. Before you buy your ticket, though, remember your history—the mantra of the mega-church is the same as of the shipping company that built the Titanic.

How did the Church lose its way?

And how—if ever—can it find the way to enough?

His Story

The story of Jesus is a different story. The story of Jesus chronicles a way of peace, not war; a way of love, not hate; compassion, not cruelty. When Jesus taught his followers to love their enemies, he illustrated that teaching with his life. On the night he was taken captive, Peter pulled a sword and cut off the ear of one of his captors. Jesus not only told his follower to put away the sword, he picked up the severed ear and put it back on the wounded man's head, healing him.

The only blood Jesus allowed shed "in his name" was his own.

Let me say that again so it will be clear to all Christians and all who aren't.

The only blood Jesus allowed shed "in his name" was his own.

That is who he was, who he is, and who he will always be. He is the Lamb of God, not a wolf in sheep's clothing; the Prince of Peace, not of politics; the wonderful counselor, not the crusader.

That is *his* story.

In the three centuries after Jesus, crosses of his impaled followers lined Roman roads. Those who followed him, followed him to death. They were humiliated, persecuted, tortured, and put on display in the most gruesome of ways in public arenas to the cheers of Roman audiences, thirsting for blood.

When Christianity became the state-sponsored religion of the Roman Empire, you would think those Christians would have kept following Jesus down the path he had blazed for them—loving their enemies, praying for those who persecuted them, blessing those who cursed them. But instead of turning the other cheek, they took to the streets. They tore down pagan temples, killed their priests, and purged the land of infidels. The persecuted became the persecutors.

How, for the love of God, did it happen?

It happened the same way it happens today.

It happens when we don't believe that Jesus alone is enough. It happens when we believe that we have to have political influence, more seats in Congress, more votes. It happens when we believe we have to have money, the more the better, in order to advance the Kingdom of God. It happens when we believe we have to have power, and in every sphere of influence, from the city council to the Supreme Court. It happens when we believe that we have to get more people. More buildings so those people can come together. And *better* buildings so we can attract *better* people, richer people, more influential people. After all, to do more, we have to have more.

This has been the math that Christianity has used over the centuries. The formula is: Jesus plus something = more than Jesus alone. The "something" is different in each generation, but though the variable is different, the formula is the same.

I lived that formula most of my life.

Until I did the math.

I urge you to do the math, too.

Jesus plus something doesn't increase him, it diminishes him. It isn't more; it is less. Because implicit in the plus sign is that Jesus alone isn't enough.

Somewhere along the way, I lost my way. Why? Because I didn't believe Jesus was enough. Somewhere along the way, Christianity lost its way, too. Why? Because it didn't believe Jesus was enough either. The Church wanted more—more converts, more land, more money, more power. And with tragic results, the consequences of which we are living with to this day.

Someone once said that when the Church and State embraced, the result was infidelity. Which makes me wonder. How different would history have been if Constantine had embraced Jesus instead of Christianity? How different would the Church have been if it had embraced a carpenter instead of an empire?

How different would *we* be, you and I, if *we* had embraced him?

Your Story

What is *your* history? And how did it begin? Who did you follow, and why? Or maybe the question should be, *what* did you follow, and why? Where has that road taken you, and how do you feel about where you are now?

Somewhere in your past and in mine, a road diverged

in the wood that was our life. Then it forked. The well-traveled way leading one direction. The less-traveled one leading another. Which did *you* choose? It makes a difference. If Robert Frost was right, it makes *all* the difference.

In the Upper Room, shortly before Jesus was captured, interrogated, and tortured to death, one of his followers asked where he was going. Show us the way, he said, so we can follow you.

Jesus responded by saying, "*I* am the way."

He didn't say a religion was the way. Or a certain sect within that religion. He didn't say a creed was the way. Or a set of spiritual exercises. He said *he* was the way. *He* is the road less-traveled. An uncertain road to follow at times, I'll give you that, even a perilous road. But it is a true road, he told his disciples, and a road brimming with life.

As Jesus walked the fragrant shores of Galilee, people came and saw, came and listened, came and followed. There were no conditions to follow him. No doctrinal statement you had to sign off on. No pledge you had to commit to. You weren't flagged for your ethnicity or refused for your morality. Your sex didn't qualify you or disqualify you; neither did your standing in the community. His appeal was simple.

> "Are you tired? Worn out? Burned out on religion? Come to me. Get away with me and you'll recover your life. I'll show you how to take a real rest. Walk with me and work with me—watch how I do it. Learn the unforced rhythms of grace. I won't lay anything heavy or ill fitting on you. Keep company with me and you'll learn to live freely and lightly." (The Message)

To those hunched over their nets or their accounting tables, to those who were worn out and burned out on religion, Jesus said "Come." To those of us who are hunched over our desks or our computer tables, those of us who are worn out and burned out, he says, "Come."

He doesn't say come to Christianity. He doesn't say come to Church. He says come *to me*.

What he offers when we come is recovery.

Recovery of the life we have lost along the way . . . the rhythms we have lost along the way . . . the freedom and the lightness we have lost along the way.

He calls us not to a guilt trip but to a getaway.

This is *his* way, a way largely without words and certainly without swords.

When I came off the withdrawal from my addiction to religion, I looked at this Jesus, this one who for so long had been unknown to me. And I listened to him, this one who for so long I had turned a deaf ear to.

"Come to me," he said, smiling. And I came.

As I followed him, I came to know him. As I came to know him, I came to love him. In loving him I realized he was enough, realized *I* was enough. Just as I am. Without one plea. And without one performance.

It is *this* Jesus I want you to come and see . . . the one I have followed along the shores of the past several years . . . and from whom I have learned the unforced rhythms of grace.

He was my rest and my recovery.

Come and see.

Perhaps he will be yours.

Part I

missing the point

CHAPTER 1

Is Jesus Plus Nothing Enough?

Is Jesus plus nothing enough?

Take all the time you need. A lot is at stake. As you consider the question, let me share some thoughts throughout the course of this book that I hope will be helpful for all. For it's a question we all have to answer. But I can't answer it for you. And you can't answer it for me.

Each of us has to answer it not with a word, or with a signature, or with a vote.

We have to answer it with our lives.

It is perhaps the only question that matters.

For the answer will determine not only the course of your life but the quality of your life.

Jesus made it clear that he was enough. His revolutionary call has always been, "Follow me!" What he is saying is that the call is not to follow a religious system or a set of rules, whether it's his or anybody else's.

"Follow ME!"

It's not about following propaganda. It's not about following a program. It's about following a person. This is what sets Jesus apart from all other great leaders. He stands out by embodying his teachings. Truth is not a principle or proposition or set of beliefs. It is a person who calls all of us into relationship. Jesus didn't just *teach* the truth; he *is* the truth. He doesn't call us to simply know *things*, but to know *him*. He teaches us to be *with him*. Not to walk in lockstep with everything he said, without doubts or questions or confusion. But to walk alongside him, to watch and to learn. To keep company with him, to rest and to recover. To walk in rhythm with him, which is a graceful rhythm, not a forceful one. He doesn't weigh us down with the law. He lightens our load with his love. And step-by-step with him, day by day with him, we will learn to live freely and lightly.

Jesus' first step in introducing this new lifestyle was to gather a small circle of men. His purpose wasn't to form a focus group to clarify his message. It wasn't to form a strategic planning committee to figure out the best way to get that message to the masses. It was to gather a few followers around him, simply to be with him (Mark 3). *Just* him.

Apparently Jesus thought that he alone was enough.

Within that circle of twelve close friends, three were the closest—Peter, James, and John. When Jesus took those three up on the mountain to pray, he was fully revealed to them, transfigured into a bright flash of lightning from head to toe. At this amazing moment, Moses and Elijah appeared in glorious splendor, talking with Jesus. When the three disciples saw this, Peter wanted to put up three shelters—one for Jesus, one for Moses, and one for Elijah. The instant he suggested it, a cloud appeared, covering them with glory and filling them with fear. A voice came from the cloud, saying, "This is my son, whom I have chosen; listen to him." When the voice had spoken, they found that Jesus was alone. Moses, the Lawgiver, and Elijah, the Prophet, had vanished and all that was left was Jesus, simply and solely Jesus (Luke 9).

Apparently the Father felt that Jesus alone was enough.

When John the Baptist saw Jesus at the Jordan River, he told the crowds that he was the Lamb of God and that he was not worthy even to untie the thong on the sandals of Jesus' feet.

Apparently he felt that Jesus alone was enough.

And while John was in prison, plagued with doubts,

he sent his disciples to ask Jesus, "Are you the one who was to come, or should we expect someone else?"

Jesus replied to those disciples, "Go back and report to John what you hear and see: The blind receive sight, the lame walk, those who have leprosy are cleansed, the deaf hear, the dead are raised, and the good news is proclaimed to the poor. Blessed is anyone who does not stumble on account of me" (Matthew 11).

John's faith was affirmed by none other than Jesus himself, assuring him that he was indeed the coming one, and that he was enough.

After the resurrection of Jesus, his disciples were despondent and went back to fishing in the Sea of Galilee. Peter was especially feeling a sense of guilt because of his repeated denials of Jesus back in Jerusalem. What must have been most hurtful was that Jesus warned him of his defection. Peter's response was to declare his allegiance, vowing never to do such a thing. But when he was identified that night by a small crowd around a campfire, he sweated from the fear of being handed over to the authorities, and he buckled under the peer pressure.

That would seem the end of Peter's story. And it would have been if he had been a pastor of a contemporary church or a leader of a para-church organization. You would think his failure as a follower would have been grounds for dismissal. You would think his defection would have disqualified him. But notice how Jesus handled the situation.

Peter, along with several other defectors, fled to the Sea of Galilee, hoping to find solace in the familiar lapping of the waves, or at least a distraction from their pain by going fishing. That is just where Jesus shows up, not in the synagogue but on the shore, where *they* were. And he made them *breakfast*. Can you imagine what Peter was thinking? His guilt level must have been high, expecting Jesus to confront him with, "I told you so, Peter." But he didn't do that.

As they ate breakfast together, all were quiet. I'm sure

21

they were fearful of what Jesus might be thinking and what he was going to say. After they finished the meal, Jesus turns to Peter. Can't you sense the tension? *What will he say?* they must have wondered. And none more so than Peter.

"Peter, do you love me?"

What a shock those words must have been. Peter was expecting a lecture on duty, perhaps, and how he failed at that duty. Failed as a follower. Failed as a friend. But Jesus doesn't talk to him about duty. Rather, he talks to him about devotion. Jesus has only one concern, and it's not about responsibility, but relationship. He wanted to know Peter's heart and where it stood in relation to him. Jesus wanted to give Peter a chance to declare his relationship with him, openly and without fear. A *second* chance. And as if that isn't shocking enough, Jesus repeats the question, giving him another opportunity to publicly declare his devotion.

"Do you love me?"

"Do you love me?"

Jesus was trying to make a point with his most devoted followers. And the point is this: He is not concerned with their screw-ups or their shortcomings; he is only concerned with their relationship with him (John 21). Jesus is trying to make the same point with you and with me. Our relationship with him is enough, he's saying. *I am safe, warm, and welcoming, no matter what you've done or haven't done. You can come to me, without fear.*

I am enough, he was then saying to his followers.

I am enough, he is now saying to you and to me.

If you doubt what Jesus is saying implicitly through that passage, look what Jesus said about himself explicitly earlier in that gospel.

"I AM the bread of life. Whoever comes to me will never go hungry, and whoever believes in me will never be thirsty" (John 6).

"I AM the light of the world. Whoever follows me

will never walk in darkness, but will have the light of life" (John 8).

"I AM the gate; whoever enters through me will be saved" (John 10).

"I AM the shepherd of the sheep" (John 10).

"I AM the way, the truth and the life" (John 14).

"I AM the resurrection and the life. Anyone who believes in me will live, even though they die; and whoever lives by believing in me will never die. Do you believe this" (John 11)?

"I AM the true vine" (John 15).

When Jesus taught about the dynamic relationship he wanted with his disciples, he used the illustration of the vine and the branches. He clearly taught in this section that the relationship he wants and the only one that matters is for the disciples (the branches) to cling to and stay connected to Jesus (the vine). He even went further to say, "Without me you can do nothing." *Nothing.* What don't we understand about *nothing?* How much clearer could Jesus have said it?

Clearly in this passage, and from the other I AM passages, Jesus believed that he alone was enough.

Now, from the point of view of those Jesus touched or simply encountered, it's clear that to them Jesus plus nothing else is enough. At the birth of Jesus there is no doubt his mother, Mary, the astronomers from the East, and the shepherds in the fields of Bethlehem all believed this was the most special baby ever to have been born.

There is quite a lineup of people who came later, all believing that Jesus plus nothing else was enough. John the Baptist (Matthew 3:1-17), Nicodemus (John 3:1-21). Joseph of Arimathaea (Luke 23:50-53). The woman at the well (John 4:3-42). The sinful woman with the expensive perfume (Luke 7:36-50). The boy with the fish and loaves (John 6:1-15). The woman caught in adultery (John 8:1-11). The thief on the cross (Luke 23:40-43). And the soldier at the cross (Luke 23:47). To name just a few.

Here are a few others.

The two men who experienced the healing touch of Jesus from a distance. The Roman Centurion's servant (Matthew 8:5-13), and the nobleman's daughter (4:46-54). They were both convinced, even before the healings, that Jesus alone was enough.

Those who were tormented by evil spirits certainly knew that Jesus was enough.

The demoniac in the synagogue (Mark 1:21-28), for example, and the demoniac in Gadara (Mark 5:1-20).

Those who were blind and given back their sight believed Jesus was enough. The blind men in Jericho (Matthew 20:29-34). The blind man in Bethsaida (Mark 8:22-26). And the man born blind (John 9:1-41).

All who experienced Jesus' power of raising the dead believed he was enough.

Jairus experienced the resurrection of his daughter (Mark 5:21-43). Certainly he believed that Jesus was enough. Lazarus would also say that Jesus was enough, and his sisters, Mary and Martha, would wholeheartedly agree (John 11:1-44). Finally, the widow of Nain, whose only son was resurrected by Jesus, surely she believed that Jesus was enough (Luke 7:11-17).

All who experienced the healing touch of Jesus believed he was enough. Peter's mother-in-law, for example (Matthew 8:14-17). The leper (Matthew 8:1-4). The woman who had been bleeding for 12 years (Mark 5:21-43). The paralytic who was lowered through the roof to see Jesus (Mark 2:1-12). The lame man who waited by the pool of Bethesda (John 5:2-15). The man with the withered hand who showed up at the synagogue (Matthew 12:9-21). The woman whose back was so bent that she was bent over permanently (Luke 13:10-17). The man with dropsy (Luke 14:1-6).

Although only one expressed his gratefulness to

Jesus, all ten lepers experienced the truth that Jesus' word was enough (Luke 17:11-19). The Syrophoenician woman who begged for her daughter to be healed (Luke 15:21-28). The lame man outside Jerusalem, healed in the name of Jesus (Acts 3). Jesus' early disciples believed that Jesus plus nothing else was enough. (Matthew 9:9-13, Luke 24:13-35, Acts 9). To make sure the point of his life didn't get lost, Jesus re-iterated it to those who had been with him. Before Jesus ascended into heaven, he presented himself to his disciples and gave them many convincing proofs that he was alive. He appeared to them over a period of forty days and taught them about the kingdom of God (Acts 1). What was most important to Jesus was that his early disciples get to know him better—to hang out with him. Jesus was again making the point that he alone is enough—knowing him and his Kingdom principles was the theme of his final 40 days.

Not only did Jesus make this point; his disciples were examples of this point.

After Peter healed a lame man, the religious leaders confronted him and John, warning them to stop this talk about Jesus. But when they saw the courage of Peter and John, realizing that they were unschooled, ordinary men, they were astonished. And they took note that these men had been *with Jesus* (Acts 4). The religious leaders didn't see the organizational affiliation of these men. They saw their *relational* affiliation. The leaders saw something in these disciples that was just Jesus. They saw that the Jesus who had been with them, now lived in them and through them. Where did the disciples get that life? From being connected to the vine. All the love and forgiveness and life that flowed through that vine to them, flowed through them to give life to others.

Paul and Timothy wrote about their relationship with Jesus, too. After listing all of his educational, religious, and moral accomplishments, Paul says, "But whatever were

25

gains to me I now consider loss for the sake of Jesus the Christ. What is more, I consider everything a loss because of the surpassing worth of knowing Jesus, for whose sake I have lost all things. I consider them garbage (manure, dung, or s#*t), that I may gain him" (Philippians 3).

Certainly Paul believed that Jesus alone is enough.

In another letter written to the Corinthians by Paul and Sosthenes, they say, "But I am afraid that, as the serpent deceived Eve by his craftiness, your minds will be led astray from the simplicity and purity of devotion to Christ"(2 Corinthians 11).

It's about relationship, not religion, Paul is saying. It's about devotion, not doctrine. Affiliation with him, not with an organization.

Jesus alone is enough.

It's that simple.

That pure and that simple.

If Jesus presented himself as enough, and those he touched believed he was enough, why do we miss this point, which is the very essence of the Good News of Jesus?

We are able to develop entire belief systems around Jesus, enlist the masses to join our organizations around Jesus, judge those who do not quite see eye-to-eye with us about Jesus, and propagate these belief systems, organizations and dogma as the only way to life, yet all without getting to know this Jesus personally.

How is it that we can miss that Jesus is enough?

There are three subtle ways this occurs, in my opinion.

First, there is a tendency to add something unnecessary to Jesus. This "something" takes the form of manmade commandments and long-standing traditions; in other words, Jesus with additives (Mark 7).

Second, there is a tendency to hold something sacred that has become a substitute for Jesus. These substitutes can be your sacred scriptures, your revered saints, your religious services, your particular organization or denomination, your cultural identification or religious icons.

Third, there is a tendency to leave Jesus behind. Whether it is in newsletters, religious services, sermons, articles, prayers, or worship experiences, Jesus is embarrassingly left behind! Even where two are three are gathered together in his name, he is so often left out of our conversations.

These tendencies take away from the message of Jesus. They diminish Jesus by adding something unnecessary to him, by replacing him with something, and by leaving him and his message behind. These tendencies amount to a deadly triad that keeps us from seeing Jesus clearly.

If we can't see him, how will we ever be able to know him? And if we can't know him, how will we ever be able to know if he is enough?

Back to my original question. It's not one I am pressing you to answer. It's one I'm simply pressing you to consider. You've taken a look at Jesus, what he said, what he did. You've taken a look at what others thought about him, said about him. You've come and you've seen. Where are you in your thinking?

The conclusion to this chapter I've adapted from part of Chip Brogden's essay, *"Is Jesus Enough."* Read through it slowly. Reflecting on the state of things in your religious circle. Reflecting on the state of things in your soul…

> *When apostles love church planting and mission work more than Jesus,*
> *they are saying that Jesus is not enough.*

27

When prophets love their prophecies, dreams, and visions more than they love Jesus,
>*they are saying that Jesus is not enough.*

When evangelists love traveling, preaching, and meetings more than they love Jesus,
>*they are saying that Jesus is not enough.*

When pastors love church services and building programs more than they love Jesus,
>*they are saying that Jesus is not enough.*

When teachers love their teachings more than they love Jesus,
>*they are saying that Jesus is not enough.*

When preachers love their preaching more than they love Jesus,
>*they are saying that Jesus is not enough.*

When ministers love their ministry more than they love Jesus,
>*they are saying that Jesus is not enough.*

When musicians love their music more than they love Jesus,
>*they are saying that Jesus is not enough.*

When writers love their writings more than they love Jesus,
>*they are saying that Jesus is not enough.*

>*When any of us grow tired of "just" being with Jesus, longing for something bigger, something better, something greater, something more powerful, something other than what we have in Jesus already,*
>>*we are saying that Jesus is not enough.*

>*How about you?*
>*If Jesus were all you had,*
>*would he be enough?*

CHAPTER 2

Are "Liar, Lunatic, Lord" Our Only Options?

Get away with me for four years, and I'll make sure you are educated beyond your intelligence. Your mind will be filled with answers, and your heart will be filled with arrogance. Come to me all you who are resting in grace and I'll weary you with law. Come to me all you who live freely and lightly, and I will lay a burden on you so heavy it will weigh you down, let you down, and eventually bring you down.

No, those aren't the words of Jesus.

The words, however, reflect the reality of my experience at seminary.

The goal of the seminary was "Preach the Word." The curriculum was structured around that goal. And so we had courses on every book of the Bible, in English, in Hebrew, and in Greek. We also had courses on preaching. Along with that, we had biblically-based courses on systematic theology—pneumatology, ecclesiology, soteriology, eschatology, and so forth.

Before we could be admitted to follow that course of study, though, we had to get past the seminary's gatekeepers. We had to have the grades, the SAT scores, the letters of recommendation, the written personal testimony. And, we had to be able to sign off on all the points and sub-points of the seminary's doctrinal statement. Once accepted, we had a heavy yoke of requirements put on our shoulders. We had to pay our tuition, buy our books, read the books we had bought, go to class, listen to lectures, take exams, write papers, and, as a final rite of passage, write a master's thesis. Upon successful completion of that check-list, we were awarded a diploma for a Th.M.—Master of Theology.

It was an arduous apprenticeship. Four years. One hundred twenty hours of course credits. We had to declare a major early on, from Old Testament Literature and Exegesis to Church History to a plethora of others. The curriculum ranged from courses in Bible Study Methods to Biblical Archeology, a long list of required courses, along with a list of electives.

I met a lot of faculty members in seminary, a lot of students, visiting lecturers, chapel speakers. All of them well-educated. Many of them skilled exegetes and eloquent expositors. Some with keen insights, fascinating stories, and successful ministries. I met a lot of wonderful people there.

But I didn't meet Jesus.

Regrettably, there wasn't a major offered on following him. In fact, in all the courses that were offered, only one was offered on "The Life and Times of Jesus."

Perhaps that is why all of us there—students as well as faculty—missed the point.

There just wasn't room for him there. Not in the curriculum. Not in the classroom. Not in our conversations.

The inn was full.

After graduating, I was launched into the world with diploma in hand, principles in tow, answers in mind, and an air of arrogance that is captured in this saying that a lot of faculty believe—"You can always tell a Dallas man . . . but you can't tell him much."

There is a lot of truth to that. It is an ironic truth, though, and ultimately a tragic truth. You certainly couldn't tell *me* much, because by that time I wasn't all that teachable. *I* was the teacher, the expert, the sought-after consultant. *I* was the one with the answers. *I* was the one with the gifts, the training, the charisma.

I was successful right out of the chute. Wildly successful. But it wasn't enough. It was never enough. And so I just kept adding more onto my schedule, onto my list of responsibilities, onto my accomplishments. Over time, though, the burden of more weighed me down, let me down, and finally brought me down.

That's when I met Jesus. He was different than I expected. He was different from the Christian faculty that educated me, different from the Christian crowds that flocked around me, different from the Christian friends that deserted me.

Jesus was the one who stayed. He was the one who didn't shake his head in disappointment, didn't turn away in disgust. He is the one who knelt down, picked me up, dusted me off. He is the one who embraced me. It was then I realized that the Jesus I had first embraced was different from the one who was embracing me now.

And I realized something else.

That Jesus I could follow.

That Jesus I wanted to follow, needed to follow, couldn't help but follow.

Not the Jesus who is wrapped up in a religious system of do's and don'ts. Not the Jesus who is used to raise money to build more and more buildings or fill the religious treasuries. Not the Jesus who was highjacked for the violent Crusades . . . persecuting, killing, even mass-murdering Jews, Muslims, all non-Christians, and even other Christians who disagreed with them. Not the Jesus who is embraced by a political candidate or party to impress the people. Not the Jesus who wants you to join his club. Not the Jesus who puts a heavy guilt trip on you for not performing. Not the hellfire-and-damnation Jesus. Nor the meek-and-mild Jesus.

This Jesus is the one I never really knew. The one

without Christian verbiage. The one without religious baggage. The one without self-righteous garbage.

This is Jesus plus nothing.

This Jesus is the Jesus that the early followers, called disciples, got to know. For three-and-a-half years they were in an apprentice relationship with Jesus. In their system of education they never made the grade of being chosen by a rabbi to follow in his steps, so they had returned home to work the family business. But this rabbi, this Jesus, this new guy in town, he chooses them to follow him. He picked uneducated, untrained, ordinary men to come along with him and learn from him. In a sense, Jesus chose those who hadn't made the cut, walk-ons, as the team he wanted on the field in the most important game in the history of the world.

From those early beginnings, the Jesus movement continues to be the largest in the world today. This all-encompassing movement consists of people from every culture and religion on the earth—Christians, Muslims, Buddhists, Jews, Hindus, Sikhs, Pantheists, Agnostics. When Jesus is not boxed into any religious system or wrapped up in a package marked "exclusive," he has proven to be universally attractive throughout the world. People from every culture embrace Jesus, simply Jesus, whether religious or not.

Take Gandhi, for example. He was so captivated with the life and teachings of Jesus that he became one of the greatest followers of Jesus ever. One of the most common descriptions of Gandhi was that he was so "Christ-like." Gandhi discovered that his cultural background as a Hindu was enhanced by Jesus. "I shall say to Hindus," he once said, "that your life will be incomplete unless you reverentially study the teachings of Jesus. . . . Make this world the kingdom of God and his righteousness and everything will be added unto you." Gandhi, whose goal in life was to live the Sermon on the Mount, said, "It was that sermon that has endeared Jesus to me." And, about Jesus' death on the cross, he said: "A man who was completely innocent, offered himself as a sacrifice for the good of others, including his enemies, and became the ransom of the world. It was a perfect act."

And finally the quote that was probably his most famous: "I like your Christ. I do not like your Christians. They are so unlike your Christ."

The current Dalai Lama is another example. He has expressed his love and respect for Jesus in many ways and on many occasions. Many of his teachings reflect those of Jesus. As the example and leader of the Buddhist community, the Dalai Lama is called His Holiness, yet he says he is not worthy to even untie the shoes of Jesus. In an OP-ED article he once wrote for *The New York Times,* the Dalai Lama wrote: "In my readings of the New Testament, I find myself inspired by Jesus' acts of compassion. His miracle of the loaves and fishes, his healing, and his teaching are all motivated by the desire to relieve suffering."

Both Gandhi and the Dalai Lama revere Jesus as the greatest teacher and example who ever lived.

Looking at the long history of Jewish thought, some of the most prominent rabbis have come to revere Jesus as possibly the most influential Jew who ever lived. Dr. David Flusser, in his book, *The Sage From Galilee: Rediscovering Jesus' Genius,* broke down many barriers that have kept Jews from studying Jesus. Albert Einstein, one of the greatest scientists in the world said this about Jesus: "As a child I received instruction both in the Bible and in the Talmud. I am a Jew, but I am enthralled by the luminous figure of the Nazarene. . . . No one can read the Gospels without feeling the actual presence of Jesus. His personality pulsates in every word."

Unfortunately, though, when Jews attempt to study the life and teachings of Jesus, they do so with the weight of history pushing against them. The Jewish people have been so persecuted by people who have called themselves Christians throughout history—from the Crusades to the Holocaust (Hitler was very public about his Christianity)—that it is extremely difficult for them to see Jesus clearly.

Most Christians are unaware that the Muslim holy book, the Qur'an, refers to Jesus more times than it does Mohammed. Prophet Jesus, known as Isa, is held up as the only supernatural Prophet. The Prophet Jesus is presented as the miracle worker, the "Word of God," the "clear sign of God," born of a virgin, alive today, and coming back to bring peace on earth. Jesus is also identified as the "ruhalla"—the only one originating from the Spirit of God (Allah). Jesus is viewed as the most unique One, Who was articulated in the Injil (the Gospels of the Bible).

But when Muslims attempt to study the life and teachings of Jesus, they do so with the weight of history against them, too. The ugly history of the Crusades still lingers today. Add to this ugliness the hateful narrative from extremists within the Christian and Muslim communities and you can see why Jesus can become so distorted.

Agnostics are another group of people who have many in their ranks who follow Jesus. In my experience they are perhaps the most open to Jesus when he is presented without all the religious baggage. Agnostics have a vacuum in their hearts. In my experience, this seems to be a God-shaped vacuum. I continually enjoy conversing with agnostics, once I am able to convince them that I don't want to discuss religion. It seems that this group is better able to view Jesus separated from the religious wrappings. They've already rejected the religious trappings and were left empty. But, when introduced to Jesus without religious baggage, so often they respond by saying: "I can follow *this Jesus!*"

The "self-help movement" is another group of people who revere Jesus, some going as far as to follow him. Even in our highly educated, secularized society, the principles of Jesus are the basis for most of the self-help and motivational principles. Though they may not use his name, they do use his teaching and his example.

In many ways this is nothing new. Jesus has always worked with people from every culture and found them to be attracted to him. The problem in the First Century was the religious jealousy of the "gatekeepers" of Judaism. When Jesus presented his message of love and compassion to the non-religious and to all other non-Jewish nations of the world, he was resisted, ridiculed, and ultimately rejected.

Why?

Jesus was a threat to their holy huddle.

Sound familiar?

The Most Common Obstacle to Following Jesus

I want to share with you what I believe to be the most common obstacle that discourages people from following Jesus. The obstacle revolves around the popular, almost sacred question: "Is Jesus a liar, a lunatic, or is he Lord?"

He doesn't fit the profile of a liar. He certainly isn't a lunatic. He *must* be Lord.

The logic is irrefutable.

I embraced this logic and taught it for many years to thousands of people. I drew a chart illustrating these three options and said, "Most people avoid these options and think of Jesus as a good teacher or a great example." Then I would move into my most dogmatic voice and say, "He didn't leave that alternative to us! Jesus was either the Lord, a liar, or he was nuts!"

I made fun of anyone who couldn't see this. Then, I'd invite people to accept Jesus as Lord. (I mean, really, who wants to say that Jesus is a liar or a lunatic?) I was really forcing them into this decision by the process of elimination. This happens over and over. People are forced to choose Jesus as Lord! Just as Charlemagne forced the Muslims at the river to choose Jesus as *their* Lord.

Though we don't use lethal force to get a person to make that choice, we often use emotional force or peer pressure. How do we do this? By having people go forward to the altar. By having them pray a prescribed prayer. By encouraging them to stand and say, "I believe!" By suggesting they throw a stick in a campfire. So, by some active response, a person must choose to believe that Jesus is Lord. Whether he knows Jesus or not. Whether he understands what that means or not. I excluded so many who couldn't make the jump over the hurdle to believe Jesus was Lord.

Most people don't take a running start and leap like a long jumper into accepting Jesus as Lord. Most people can't do that. Most of us come to Jesus in steps. And we follow him in steps, too.

What I should have said to them is what Philip said to Nathaniel or the woman at the well said to the people in her village: "Come and see."

Check Out Jesus

Jesus himself never pressured anyone with these tent revival tactics.

He never required anyone to believe he was Lord.

He never required anyone to believe he was the Son of God.

He never required anyone to believe he was the Messiah.

That just wasn't his approach.

His approach was simply, "Come."

"Come to me" . . . "come and follow" . . . "come and rest" . . . "come and learn."

So why do so many insist on placing hurdles in the way of people checking Jesus out?

Check Out His Early Followers

Jesus' early followers were curious about Jesus, impressed with his teaching, and drawn to his example. As they followed him, they heard and saw wonderful things, amazing things even. They heard him give the Sermon on the Mount. They saw him change water into wine. They watched as he healed the sick, fed the hungry. They were highly responsive to him at first, but they weren't very strong believers at the beginning of the journey. But step by step, they came closer to him, saw more, heard more. And step-by-step, they were changing, something was stirring in them. The kindness of God. The Kingdom of God. Such wonderful things, new things, life-giving things.

You see, there are lots of people, maybe you are one of them, who are just where the disciples were in the beginning—curious, fascinated, interested in this Jesus; impressed even.

When I tell an interested agnostic that he is exactly like the early disciples of Jesus, he or she is taken aback. But this is true! They are leaning in to get to know more about Jesus. What happens to this interest if the door is shut in their faces, by forcing them to believe certain things without examination?

So Who Can Follow Jesus?

In a word—anyone!

And *how* can we follow him?

There seem to be three progressive stages of

following Jesus.

First—People follow Jesus because he is genuine and winsome. He is the one person who has truly walked the walk, and walked it perfectly. No one argues with this. There is nothing wrong with this type of following Jesus at all. This is following the pattern of the early disciples or followers.

Second—As people continue to follow this winsome and attractive Jesus, many begin to resonate with his life— the way he talks, the things he says, the way he treats people. They resonate with his love, his compassion, his gentleness, his mercy. Something inside them resonates with the truth of his teachings, the simplicity of his illustrations, and the sincerity of his spirit. They find Jesus not only practical and meaningful to their lives, they find him admirable and exemplary.

Third—As people continue to follow this Jesus and find his teachings meaningful, they may come to the point of realizing he is more than just another human. Many find peace through Jesus—peace within them and peace with others. Many find a joy that continues, no matter what's happening around them. Many find Jesus as a reference point, bringing them balance and perspective. Many find a hope in Jesus that gets them through the trials in life. Many find Jesus satisfies their deepest longings and dreams. Many find Jesus as someone to talk to and get real answers impressed in their hearts. Many see Jesus as a great prophet. Many see Jesus as God with skin on.

The continuum of following Jesus is illustrated best in an encounter Jesus had with Peter and his early followers in a place called Caesarea Philippi. They have been following this attractive, irresistible, and relevant Jesus for quite some time and now the question comes from Jesus: "Who do you say I am?"

Peter's answer was, "You are the Messiah, the Son of the living God." This is the first time this has been expressed with a sense of conviction by these followers. The thought was there, but this seems to nail it down. They believed Jesus was God's Messiah, the Son of the living God. Now note Jesus' reply to Peter's answer. He first says, "Blessed are you, Simon, son of Jonah." Jesus strokes Peter for expressing this answer to the question. But before Peter gets too puffed up for coming up with this great answer, Jesus quickly says, "This was not revealed to you by flesh and blood."

He is saying, "Peter, you didn't think this up on your own and no one taught you this truth." Did you get this? No one can teach this kind of thing to you. There is no set of doctrines or beliefs that can bring you to this point. Jesus goes on to explain, "but by my Father in heaven." God revealed this to you, Peter.

Why did God reveal this to him?

Because he had been following after this Jesus for years.

So Again, Who Can Follow Jesus?

Wherever you are in this continuum of the stages in following Jesus, *anyone, anywhere* can start following after this Jesus.

Can you see that anyone can start following Jesus, no matter what he or she believes, no matter their cultural background, religious background, social-economic background, or moral background?

Can you see how Christians, Muslims, Jews, Hindus, Buddhists, Sikhs, Agnostics, or whatever a person's bent, may start following Jesus at any point of understanding?

Once an atheist, and a very closed-minded one at that, Oxford professor and critic, C. S. Lewis became a follower of Jesus. Reluctantly at first, by his own admission. But he saw enough of this winsome Jesus to take a halting step. One after the other. Until at last he started thinking differently, living differently, teaching differently, and writing differently. He went from writing essays on literary criticism to the *Chronicles of Narnia*. And he remained a follower to the end of his life.

When Lewis was an atheist, he made the statement, "How absurd that a human could possibly believe that he could have a personal relationship with the Creator God." He said, "It is as absurd as Hamlet thinking he could have a personal relationship with Shakespeare, his creator."

Later, on further thought, Lewis observed, "Hamlet could have had a personal relationship with Shakespeare, if Shakespeare had written himself, the author/creator, as a character into the play."

This is what I believe God did.

He wrote himself into the play.

The name of the character?

Jesus.

Come and See

Consider this Jesus who is revered as:
>the Christ to Christians;
>a rabbi to the Jews;
>a prophet to the Muslims;
>an avatar to the Hindus;
>an enlightened one to Buddhists;
>a wise teacher to secularists;
>a friend to the broken and disenfranchised.

However they view him, however *you* view him . . . his name is Jesus. And he is out to deliver the message of good news to all people of all religions, even to those with no religion at all. Here are three of their stories.

A story from a Buddhist:

A broken, addicted, and lost Tibetan youth, after studying Jesus three hours a day in a mentoring house said this: "My life has been changed through getting to know

Jesus. I am no longer trapped by my drugs. I have found a family here at the house and am learning to follow Jesus as my Master, even as a Buddhist."

A letter from a Hindu:

Dear Tim,

Your thoughts on Jesus have been thrilling, inspiring and encouraging! It has indeed been a fascinating journey to go through your beautifully crafted articles on Jesus. I think it is mainly because I am a Hindu who follows Jesus whole-heartedly and with joy. I accept Him as my redeemer and one and only God! I have always loved Jesus so I got to know about Him some years ago but not the Christianity. I follow His principles and words and try to live accordingly.

I agree with you that one must let his/her family know about Jesus first and then to start one to one with colleagues and gradually to reach the good news to everyone! I have been trying that because I found a great joy in doing so. My wife is still an orthodox Hindu, but she does not have a problem in loving Jesus. I am confident that one day she will have a new life in Jesus. I tell you, like many other Hindus, she does not like Christianity.

Since 1951, right after the "Ranas" downfall in Nepal, Christians started pouring into Nepal in different names to convert people into another civilization, Christianity. I think that was the serious mistake! It is just an analysis, perhaps I am wrong. Today there are just about a million Christians in Nepal (predominantly a Hindu country) but honestly telling there are very few true followers of Jesus. I wish more were here, telling people that Jesus is not only for Christians, but for all, regardless of their cultural and religious identities.

I believe you are aware that most of the pastors of the churches in this country are rich and are living a lavish life! People here call them emerging Christian businessmen as they continue to flourish with generous aid from the West. Every year thousands of dollars enters in this country in the name of building churches and serving the poor. We must pray for these brothers and sisters that they come to know Jesus and repent for what they have been doing. We also need to pray for them that they begin to follow Jesus!

A story from a Muslim family:

My wife Diana and I have had the privilege of meeting with Muslim students and other young Muslims over the years, but one of the most thrilling experiences was when we met with a Muslim family.

The women were all covered. These were serious Muslims. I shared with them that we have been diligently following Jesus and this journey led us to find Jesus in their Holy Book, the Qur'an. They knew Jesus was in the Qur'an and so they were pleased with my words. I shared with them that Jesus is the only supernatural prophet within the Qur'an, the only one who performed miracles. They readily agreed with me as I continued to tell them what we've found about Jesus in the Qur'an. (I don't think they actually knew the things I was sharing, but they nodded with enthusiastic agreement. It was from their Qur'an and they loved it that we loved what we had discovered about Jesus there.)

I continued by sharing with them that Jesus is called the "word of God" several times. Jesus was identified as the "clear sign" of God, which equates to being the "way to God." Again, they agreed with my analysis about Jesus, though I'm convinced they had never heard such things before. They also had never met anyone who was actually following Jesus, as if Jesus were actually alive and real. To them, anyone who claimed to follow Jesus in this way was a Christian who was interested in converting them to Christianity . . . *until* they met us. They loved hearing about this Jesus and are eager to talk more about this Jesus and how to follow him.

My point in sharing these stories with you is that people around the world are eager to come and see . . . not Christianity . . . not the Church . . . *Jesus.* And when you show them *just* Jesus, without all the cultural and ecclesiastical add-ons, they are drawn to him.

I come to you without credentials or qualifications, more like the woman at the well than the leader of the religious council. I come with a simple but sincere plea.

"Come see. Come see this man who can't be explained, can't be put into a box, can't be categorized, systematized, or Christianized."

It doesn't matter where you are from—Ethiopia or Samaria or Judea. It doesn't matter who you are—male or female, Jew or Gentile, slave or free. It doesn't matter what you do—tax-collector, fisherman, prostitute. It doesn't matter if you are a centurion who pledges allegiance to Caesar or a pagan who offers sacrifices at the temple of Artemis or a Pharisee who is part of a corrupt religious system.

"Come," Jesus says to you and to me and to anyone who will listen to his call by the shore.

"Come to me."

"And come as you are."

CHAPTER 3

What Were My Blinders?

Through a few close friends I realized I had missed the point of Jesus. As I look back over my life, it's as if I had a set of blinders on that kept me from seeing him. I had eyes to see, but wasn't seeing him. I had ears to hear, but wasn't hearing him. Here is how my blinders were developed.

Growing up, I was not only Christian, I was a Baptist Christian. And I was not just any kind of Baptist. I was a General Association of Regular Baptists. I attended a Christian liberal arts university. Then I made my way through the labyrinth of a four-year theological seminary. I logged seven years of Greek in order to study the New Testament. I studied three-and-a-half years of Hebrew to study the Old Testament. I learned so much there. In fact, most of what I learned I've never been able to share with anyone, because no one has asked me a question about it. This is why I say I've been educated beyond my intelligence.

Although I discovered that quite a few more are getting into heaven (even Methodists and Catholics!), very little time at seminary was given to either practical ministry training or learning how to think. A few of our teachers had a refreshing way of provoking thought, but that was rare. For the most part we were indoctrinated into a certain ideology—an unswerving theological point of view without the opportunity to question or disagree. Seminary was more like a vocational training school. Like so much of our educational experience today, the process was to take notes and burp them back up on the bluebook exam. When I was handed my diploma, I also received, unknown to me at the time, a set of Western Christian blinders.

Some of you may not know how blinders work. Have you seen those magnificent racehorses, wearing blinders on a muddy racetrack? They serve a purpose to keep the horses focused. The blinders I had received served to keep me focused, too. Focused on what I had been taught, on reading and listening to the fraternity of those who thought as we did, giving me the ability to argue our forms of Christianity, convincing me that I had the truth and that that truth must be spread.

I learned the art of add-ons. I learned how to substitute Christianity, church, and charisma for Jesus. I learned how to leave him out of most of my conversations and out of most of my life. My life was filled with Christianity. Studying it. Teaching it. Defending it. Spreading it.

Looking back, my vocational training didn't mentor me in following Jesus.

The goal was to be a good Dallas man who could be counted on to "preach the Word." With few exceptions along the way, I didn't encounter Jesus. But I did encounter Christianity, at least, my theological corner of it.

In college, I had been trained in Classical Rhetoric; in seminary, I had listened to and been mentored by the best orators there. The more I worked with my audiences, the more I grappled with people's personal problems and relational entanglements. I learned to scratch where people itched, and people itched a lot. The more they itched, the more I scratched Although the principles I was using were taught by Jesus, I presented them more subtly in the manner of self-help. I had learned to work for Jesus in an advisory capacity, even though there were no openings or positions like that available. Vocationally I was viewed as a success. Thousands were showing up every weekend. Thousands upon thousands of book sales. As many speaking engagements as I wanted. And a waiting list of people who wanted me to counsel them.

Where I Missed the Point

Fitted with my vocational blinders and living in the spotlight of my status as a Christian celebrity, I missed the point of Jesus. I couldn't see him. I missed his teachings. I missed the significance of his actions. I missed Jesus, simply Jesus.

My vocational blinders had me highly motivated to prepare a great message for the weekend "church" show. After all, if the weekend "show" (where we spent most of our budget) didn't go well, everything else suffered. As many "church" growth experts have put it: "The Sunday services must set the pace and lead the way for the entire momentum."

Therefore most of my time was not spent in preparing my heart or in researching the teachings of Jesus (I thought I already knew about Jesus!). Most of my time was spent in packaging the message in such a way to dazzle the crowd! And, it worked! They were dazzled! But most of the time, though, Jesus was left behind.

Our success seduced us. And we missed the revolutionary nature of Jesus, who had no desire of building a holy huddle and keeping it together. We came each Sunday to build the huddle, and Jesus came to break it up!

Huddle-breaking Measures

When I began to look at Jesus with a new perspective, I discovered that he made it a habit of reaching out to people from all kinds of religious and cultural backgrounds. He was inclusive, not exclusive as is so often taught. My vocational, religious blinders kept me from seeing this all-inclusive Jesus in action.

Let's examine seven encounters Jesus had with people

from other nations. These are great illustrations of how he was about breaking up holy huddles and reaching out to all cultures. Let's start with the woman at the well.

The Woman at the Well (John 4). On his way from Jerusalem to the Galilee, Jesus took a shortcut through Samaria. This was not the usual route Jews would take, because they were locked up in major tension with the Samaritans. The Jews strongly rejected the Samaritans and kept separate from them.

The reason?

Samaritans were a mixed race and not as pure as the Jews were. The animosity between the two was intense. No trust...no association...not even conversation.

While traveling through Samaria, Jesus and his disciples stopped at the well at the town of Sychar. Jesus decided to rest at the well, but his disciples went into town to shop for food. It was noon, the heat of the day, and a woman showed up to draw water. Jesus initiated a conversation with her. He asked for a drink. She was shocked that he, a Jew, would even speak to her. In the course of the conversation, he turns her attention to a special kind of water—living water. He explained that living water is different from well water. Sure, well water quenches physical thirst, but living water quenches the thirst of the soul. He tells her that this living water is so satisfying that she will never thirst again. In fact, this living water becomes a whole well of water within that springs up to eternal life. Naturally, she wanted this kind of water. Who wouldn't?

Then Jesus gets personal. He tells her to go get her husband. She said, "I have no husband." Jesus replied, "You are right. You've had five husbands and are working on the sixth!"

With this incredible insight into her life, the woman believes Jesus must be some kind of prophet. So she turns the discussion toward religion and their differences in worship. Jesus' response is unique: "Woman, believe me, a time is coming when you will not worship God in your Samaritan way nor in the Jewish way. Soon true worshipers of God will worship in spirit and in truth, not in a certain building or location. God is looking for people to seek Him this way, since God is Spirit and Truth."

The woman expressed that she knew God will be sending His Messiah and He will explain all things. That is when Jesus makes a shocking, some would say scandalous declaration: "I am he."

At that moment, the disciples show up to see their Jewish leader alone with a Samaritan woman. She quickly left for town to share this strange, yet wonderful encounter she had. She told her neighbors, "Come see a man who told me everything I ever did! Could this be the Messiah?"

The townspeople came to the well to see Jesus for themselves. They urged him to stay with them, and he stayed with them for two days. Many others believed, the text says, based on what he shared with them.

Note what happened here. Jesus shifted the discussion of well water to living water. He was interested in her and her life. Jesus already knew her and accepted her anyway. That blew her mind! Jesus wanted to show her how to be truly satisfied in a new way. He didn't argue religious or cultural differences. He pointed her to true worship of God in the heart. Jesus was not promoting any religious system. He didn't make any move to convert her to another religious system. He was offering a personal relationship with God, not an opportunity to change huddles.

***The Woman from Syrophoenicia* (Mark 7; Matthew 15).** Exhausted by the many arguments with the religious leaders, Jesus left the area for a getaway into the region of Tyre and Sidon. This is a non-Jewish area. In the home where Jesus was to stay he encountered a non-Jewish woman. Mark calls her Syrophoenician and Matthew refers to her as Canaanite. Neither was friendly to the Jews.

The Syrophoenicians or Canaanites worshiped a variety of nature gods. El was the chief god who was portrayed as a bully, and this image kept people in fear. This woman with this religious background boldly asked Jesus for help. Her daughter was tormented by evil spirits. Since her gods hadn't helped, the mother now turns to Jesus. He initially dismisses her request, but her persistence wins out.

Jesus says to her, "You have great faith! Your request is granted." Her daughter was healed that very hour. Note what happened here! Jesus honored her faith. He didn't pull her into a new religious system, didn't invite her to join a study class, didn't urge her to renounce her cultural upbringing, didn't warn her of the many man-made myths and gods of her religion.

Here's the point. This woman sought and received, and now she has her daughter whole. As a result, she went away with a special relationship with Jesus that she would never forget.

Why didn't Jesus try to convert her to the one, true God and pull her away from El or polytheism—the many gods? Why didn't Jesus invite her into the "holy huddle" of Judaism? Didn't he care about keeping the holy huddle holy? Or, at least, keeping the holy huddle a huddle?

***The Roman Centurion* (Matthew 8; Luke 7).** Check out this encounter: when Jesus had entered Capernaum, a centurion came to him, asking for help. "Lord," he said, "my servant lies at home paralyzed, suffering terribly."

Jesus said to him, "Shall I come and heal him?"

The centurion replied, "Lord, I do not deserve to have you come under my roof. But just say the word, and my servant will be healed. For I myself am a man under authority, with soldiers under me. I tell this one, 'Go,' and he goes; and that one, 'Come,' and he comes. I say to my servant, 'Do this,' and he does it."

When Jesus heard this, he was amazed and said to those following him, "Truly I tell you, I have not found anyone in Israel with such great faith."

Now, wait a minute, Jesus! This non-Jewish, Roman centurion has greater faith than you've seen in Israel? Really? But he has no religious training? How can this be?

Jesus not only pronounces a non-Jew the greatest man of faith he has seen in Israel, he rubs it in deeper. Jesus goes on to say (in Matthew's version), "Many will come to me from the east and the west and will feast with Abraham, Isaac, and Jacob in the kingdom. But the subjects of the kingdom will be thrown outside."

Those who you wouldn't think would be in God's kingdom will be. And those you would think will surely be in the kingdom will not be. Then Jesus says to the centurion, "Go! Let it be done just as you believed it would." And the centurion's servant was healed that very moment.

Note what happened here! Jesus doesn't warn the Roman centurion to avoid the many Roman gods. His concern was his faith. Jesus didn't urge this man to repent and renounce the Roman deities or his faith would not be effective.

Why is Jesus repeatedly affirming the faith of people from other nations?

Why is Jesus repeatedly exposing the lack of faith of the religious holy huddle?

The Ten Lepers (Luke 17). Now on his way to Jerusalem, Jesus traveled along the border between Samaria and Galilee. As he was going into a village, ten men who had leprosy met him. They stood at a distance and called out in a loud voice, "Jesus, Master, have pity on us!"

When he saw them, he said, "Go, show yourselves to the priests." And as they went, they were cleansed.

One of them, when he saw he was healed, came back, praising God in a loud voice. He threw himself at Jesus' feet and thanked him—and he was a Samaritan.

Jesus asked, "Were not all ten cleansed? Where are the other nine? Was no one found to return and give praise to God except this foreigner?" Then he said to him, "Rise and go; your faith has made you well."

Here we go again!

The star of this story is again a foreigner, a non-Jew, a Samaritan.

Note we see through these stories that no matter the cultural background or religion, it's the heart that impresses Jesus most. Here in the leper story it's a heart of gratefulness. No one from the Jewish holy huddle returned to give thanks to Jesus. Not one! Only the despised Samaritan.

The Royal Official's Son (John 4). A royal official whose son was dying in a nearby town approached Jesus. The official said to Jesus, "Sir, come before my child dies."

"Go," Jesus replied, "your son will live."

The man took Jesus at his word and departed. While he was still on the way, his servants met him with the news that his boy was living. When he inquired as to the time when his son got better, they said to him, "Yesterday, at one in the afternoon, the fever left him."

Then the father realized that this was the exact time at which Jesus had said to him, "Your son will live." So he and his whole household believed.

Jesus was getting more and more upset with the religious leaders of Judaism. They followed him to Galilee from Jerusalem, after seeing the miracles he performed there. This is when the royal official asked for his own miracle. Jesus said, "Unless you people see signs and wonders, you will never believe." In contrast to the religious leaders of Judaism, the royal official (the father) believed and the miracle followed.

Again, the star of this story did not belong to the holy huddle, but was an outsider, a non-Jew, from the nations of the world who had not known God.

My vocational blinders only allowed me to see this man as a person in need. I never recognized the significance of who he was in contrast to the Jews.

Feeding of the 4000 (Mark 8; Matthew 15). Often when reading about Jesus' actions, you will see that he travels back and forth from one side of the Sea of Galilee to the other. Whenever they were on the Jewish side, they crossed over to the other side. Why?

He performed the same works among the non-Jewish world as with the Jews. When Jesus was outside of the Jewish, holy huddle territory, he never urged them to change their religious culture, but let them remain right where they grew up. None of that seemed to matter to Jesus as long as they were drawn to him.

My blinders kept me from even noticing that Jesus moved back and forth from the Jews to those of other nations.

The Demonized Wild Man (Mark 5). Again, Jesus went across the lake to the other side—to the non-Jewish side. A wild-eyed demonized man who lived in the tombs met him there. He was so filled with evil spirits that no one could bind him, not even with a chain. When his hands and feet had been chained, he broke loose. No one could control him. Night and day he cried out and cut himself with stones.

Jesus commanded the evil spirits to come out of him, sending them into a herd of pigs. What a sight! He sent them into around 2000 pigs that ran off a cliff and drowned.

Note the result of this man being freed from the demons. The wild-eyed demonized man was calmed down, sitting rather than wandering around, clothed, and in his right mind. Now note the result among the people. They had been afraid of the man before, but now they were really filled with fear as they observed his miraculous transformation.

This non-Jewish, transformed man begged Jesus to let him follow along. Jesus did not let him, but said, "Go home to your own people and tell them how much the Lord has done for you, and how he has had mercy on you." Jesus had a mission for him to accomplish.

So, the man immediately went away and began sharing his story throughout all of the Decapolis, the ten Roman cities of the region. And all the people were amazed!

All seven encounters with Jesus were with people from the nations. They were not within the Jewish holy huddle. In fact, Jesus used each of these to break up the huddle and to blow up the spirit of exclusivity that tends to rise up within such huddles. That's the spirit of the holy huddle. It's us against them.

A Huddle-Breaker for Me

Several years ago I had the privilege of speaking to a very unique international gathering hosted by the Dalai Lama. More than 500 clerics—Muslim, Jewish, Hindu, Christian, and Buddhist—were invited by His Holiness to discuss peace and compassion.

The opportunity came about in a gratifying way. The group of American Buddhists who were underwriting a special event for the Dalai Lama in the United States worked with a friend of mine. One day as they were hanging out together, one of them asked, "Jack, over the last year it seems there's something different going on in your life that has given you a new sense of peace. What is it?"

Jack answered, "Well, I've been doing one of the toughest things I've ever tried to do and that is to follow the teachings and principles of Jesus."

They asked, "What church did you get this from?"

He replied, "It wasn't from a church, but from a friend—my neighbor." When he mentioned my name, one of them knew me to be a professional speaker. He asked Jack if I might be interested in speaking at this very special event. It was to be in San Francisco where the Dalai Lama was inviting hundreds of clerics from around the world to establish a multi-religious body that would work to quell violence and promote harmony between people of different faiths. Jack gave him my phone number.

When he called me, he identified himself as an American Buddhist and shared with me the purpose of the upcoming gathering. For security reasons, only the Department of State knew the exact hotel location of the event. He said, "We want to invite you to speak at this event. We have two Christians (Episcopal and Catholic) who will be representing Christianity, and we feel we need one more."

I said, "I don't have to speak. I would just love to attend this special event. Besides, I am not a good representative of Christianity. I just don't do that very well."

Stunned, my new Buddhist friend asked, "What do you represent?"

"I'm just a stubborn follower of Jesus," I replied. "He is the only one I am comfortable representing."

He sat silently on the phone for several seconds and said, "You know, I think that's better!" Quickly I said, "I do, too!" With that, I was officially invited to sit on the platform with the Dalai Lama and at some point to speak.

The *Gathering of Hearts Illuminating Compassion* was held at the Intercontinental Mark Hopkins Hotel in San Francisco. Nearly 750 gathered together, mostly clerics, respectfully awaiting His Holiness the Dalai Lama to arrive in the assembly hall. This unprecedented anti-terror summit with Muslim clerics and other religious leaders from around the world was prompted by the personal invitation of a prominent California Muslim, Imam Khorasani. Imam

Khorasani and the Dalai Lama had carved out a friendship and from that relationship wanted to communicate peace to the rest of the world. In a real sense, they wanted to help form a "United Nations of Religion," devoted to countering extremist violence.

All of the speakers were seated on the platform. I confess my anxiety level was quite high in anticipation of what I was going to say. The audience also seemed to have some anxiousness. It was in the air.

Then, the Dalai Lama entered the room from the back, along with several monks. The monks took seats on the front row, and His Holiness made his way to the platform to sit right in the middle of the speakers. When he sat down, he removed his sandals, crossed his legs, sat back and giggled as he looked out over the audience. That giggle broke the tension with his warmth and winsome smile.

The Dalai Lama opened the session with words of gratefulness to the various faiths and cultures gathered together, noting that this conference was only the beginning of many more gatherings "where we may find a gathering of hearts to bring peace to our world."

After his words of greeting, we heard from a variety of speakers (Muslim, Hindu, Jewish, Christian, and Buddhist), beginning with the well-known author of world religions, Huston Smith.

Jesus Was Missing

So many thoughts raced through my mind as to what I should say. What was most striking to me was the absence of the name of Jesus over the three hours of speakers, even from those who were designated to represent Christianity.

We were not given any idea as to the order of the

speakers, so this added to the tension I was feeling. As the program continued and we were close to the end of our time together, it was obvious that either I had been cut from the agenda or I was going to be close to the end.

After sitting on the edge of my chair throughout the entire session, I was briefly introduced. I was the last speaker of the day before His Holiness was to close our time together.

I just knew this was the best spot in the program to bring up the only one in history who could provide peace for any who wanted it. So I began with, "I bring you greetings in the name of Jesus."

The shockwave we all experienced at the mention of the name of Jesus was one of the most dramatic encounters with Jesus I've ever sensed.

I continued with, "Since Jesus is not owned by Christians or Christianity, not bound by any system of do's and don'ts, not exclusive but all-inclusive in his approach to people everywhere (He will work with anyone!), then it is appropriate to bring greetings in his name at this great event. In following Jesus I have come to realize that what the world needs now is not more love."

I paused for a moment so that the audience could digest these words, because most of what had been discussed all afternoon was the need for love in our world. After a pregnant pause, I continued, "What the world needs now is more lovers—love in action." It was obvious that the audience was in agreement.

I ended my time with, "May Jesus fill your hearts and minds with his peace, his joy, his love, his compassion, and may he bind us together in such a way that we might be contagious in making a difference through him in our world."

The applause was not just polite, but enthusiastic and animated.

As soon as the session was dismissed, clerics from all

faiths flocked to me. They each expressed their enthusiasm for hearing more about Jesus unchained by Western, cultural Christianity.

One American Buddhist rushed up to me saying, "You're going to Tibet with me!" In further conversation this same man said, "I've never heard about Jesus separated from Christianity. You know, having heard Jesus in this way, I think I see what you are saying. I would say that Jesus trumps everything!"

On that day those words were imprinted indelibly in my heart.

That day the last threads of my vocational blinders fell off.

Jesus is the point.

Jesus plus nothing.

And he trumps everything!

CHAPTER 4

What Was Israel's Blinkered Thinking?

Two questions.

Two *very* important questions, the answers to which will change everything.

One: Why was Jesus so intent on breaking up the holy huddles wherever he went?

And two: Why did he repeatedly invite those from other nations to himself?

There is a primary reason why Jesus took on the responsibility of breaking up the holy huddle of the Jews. It all goes back to father Abraham, the father of monotheism, which is the belief in one God. He is known as the friend of God and as one of the most prominent characters from the beginnings of Judaism, Christianity, and Islam. Abraham's unshakable faith and submission to the one God has served as a major inspiration and example to all three religions.

Abraham's 2-Step

According to the Scriptures, God made a covenant with Abraham, and there were two parts to it. Here is the way the passage reads in Genesis 12:2-3 of *The Message:*

> "I'll make you a great nation,
>
>> and bless you.
>
> I'll make you famous;
>
>> you'll be a blessing.
>
> I'll bless those who bless you;
>
>> those who curse you I will curse.

> All the families of the Earth
>
> will be blessed through you."

I call this the "Abrahamic 2-Step."

Step 1—God will bless the people who are faithful to Him.

Step 2—God will be a blessing to all nations of the world through His people.

In the case of the Jewish people, God was going to bless Israel as a nation as long as they were faithful to Him—specifically faithful in being a blessing to the nations of the world!

God even changed Abram's name, meaning "noble father" to Abraham, which means "the father of many nations." God wanted to bless the whole world through Abraham. God had a bigger vision for Abraham. God was looking for the salvation of the whole world through Abraham.

Abraham was to be, not only the physical father, but also the spiritual father of many nations (AKA, gentiles).

There is no word for gentile in the Hebrew or the Greek. The words that are normally translated "gentiles" are actually the words for "nations" or "cultures."

Jesus' mission was to break up the Jewish holy huddle that was stuck in Step 1. So, Jesus' encounters with people from the nations of the world were an example of how Step 2 was to be carried out—to be a blessing to the world!

The Jewish holy huddle Jesus found when he came was in a narrow-minded, rigid, inflexible, dogmatic state of mind with blinders on. Now that' a mouthful to say, so I found one word to say it all. BLINKERED! They were unable to see the big picture of what God was up to. They had ears to hear, but couldn't hear it. They had eyes to see, but couldn't see it. Why? They were into blinkered thinking! And, Jesus' early followers had a difficult time opening their eyes and ears!

Jesus Lived Out Abraham's 2-Step

In the last chapter we examined how Jesus fulfilled Step 2 of the Abrahamic 2-Step as he related to people from the nations of the world. One of the most popular stories about Jesus was when he became angry with businessmen and threw them out of the Temple.

I've always believed Jesus was upset over the "business" done in the Temple. And he was! Not just doing business there, but cheating people in the changing of money, in the selling of "more acceptable" animals for sacrifice, in selling all of the religious knickknacks available at the time. But there is more here!

Through the prophet Isaiah, God directed that the Temple was to be a "house of prayer *for all the nations* (Isaiah 56:7)." The Temple represented the very presence of God dwelling with His people. Therefore all people from every nation were to have access to Him there. This is why the Jews were directed to have a special place for non-Jews to come to the Temple to worship.

It seems Step 2 of the Abrahamic 2-Step was not a priority to the Temple authorities in the first century nor to the Jewish people in general. The "holy huddle" desired to be kept pure from any contamination. Consequently, they cleared out the Court of the Nations—the place set aside for the non-Jews to worship—and allowed the moneychangers and vendors to use this "unused" space for business.

Why not?

Being a blessing to the nations of the world was not a priority of the huddle!

I think this is the real reason for Jesus' anger! What's interesting is that we've never been taught this reason, because being a blessing to the nations of the world is still not important! Keep Jesus exclusively for yourselves and shut out the nations of the world! Let them in only through conversion to your cultural system of beliefs, but don't allow them to respond to God through their cultural lenses. Now that's BLINKERED THINKING!

Even the Temple priest who first held Jesus in his arms as a baby knew clearly why Jesus came: "For my eyes have seen your salvation, which you have prepared in the sight of *all nations:* a light for revelation to *the nations,* and the glory of your people Israel" (Luke 2). Note the coming of the Messiah was to be a global event, not for one nation but for all nations. The one was a means to the other. A light was given to Israel, and it was to be a city set on a hill, so to speak, shining as a beacon of light to all the nations. Tragically, though, they hid that light by huddling around it themselves and consequently lost sight of their global mission.

Jesus Taught Abraham's 2-Step

Jesus not only acted out Abraham's 2-Step; he taught Step 2 repeatedly! Jesus was clearly into opening the blinkered minds of those who would listen—those who might have ears to truly hear and eyes to truly see.

After Jesus healed a man with a withered hand on the Sabbath, for example, the religious leaders plotted how they might kill him. Aware of this, Jesus withdrew from that place. A large crowd followed him and he healed all who were ill. Jesus warned them not to tell others about him. Matthew says, "This was to fulfill what was spoken through the prophet Isaiah: 'Here is my servant whom I have chosen, the one I love, in whom I delight; I will put my Spirit on him, and he will proclaim justice to the *nations.* In his name the *nations* will put their hope'"(Matthew 12). Another time Jesus taught this concept was in his hometown of Nazareth. I can see it now! This was one of the most anticipated opportunities for Jesus. News of his speaking engagement rapidly spread and all had come to hear him at their local synagogue.

When Jesus shows up on the Sabbath in the synagogue, he, as a guest rabbi, was asked to recite the reading of the day. He stood up to read and the scroll of the prophet Isaiah was handed to him. Unrolling it, he found the place where it is written: "The Spirit of the Lord is on me, because he has anointed me to proclaim good news to the poor. He has sent me to proclaim freedom for the prisoners and recovery of sight for the blind, to set the oppressed free, to proclaim the year of the Lord's favor" (Isaiah 61).

The home crowd loved it! Little Jesus had made them proud. How amazing it was!

He rolled up the scroll, gave it back to the attendant and sat down. The eyes of everyone in the synagogue were fastened on him. Jesus said, "Today this scripture is fulfilled in your hearing." All spoke well of him, the text says, and were amazed at the gracious words that came from his lips.

Then the bombshell.

Jesus said, "Truly I tell you prophets are not accepted in their hometowns." He then offers two illustrations of prophets who were not welcomed and how those of other nations were blessed by their famous prophets. Elijah: Jesus says, "I assure you that there were many widows in Israel in Elijah's time, when the sky was shut for three and a half years and there was a severe famine throughout the land. Yet Elijah was not sent to any of them, but to a widow in Zarephath in the region of Sidon" (non-Jewish). In other words, God sent one of His prophets to a non-Jewish widow to comfort and care for him.

Jesus goes on to say, "And there were many in Israel with leprosy in the time of Elisha the prophet, yet not one of them was cleansed—only Naaman the Syrian" (non-Jewish). God didn't bless any Jewish lepers with healing, but he did heal a non-Jew.

The people were livid. They rose up, drove Jesus out of town, and took him to the brow of a hill to throw him off the cliff. Ironically, though, perhaps even miraculously, he slipped through the crowd and went on his way (Luke 4).

Just point out God's blessing on non-Jewish nations and watch the holy huddle squirm! I'll never forget when I introduced our Muslim friend as a follower of Jesus to a group of Palestinian Christian youths in Bethlehem. The shock and gasps around the room were amazing! Talk about squirming! But as we processed this together, they came to understand for the first time ever that Jesus is not a Christian, nor is he owned by Christians. He is the light *of the world*. Not the western world. The *whole* world. Not the Christian world. The *whole* world.

To emphasize this, Jesus talks about other sheep, outside the white wooly huddle. "I am the good shepherd; I know my sheep and my sheep know me—just as the Father knows me and I know the Father—and I lay down my life for the sheep. I have *other sheep* that are not of this sheep pen. I must bring them also. They too will listen to my voice, and there shall be one flock and one shepherd" (John 10). Who are these "other sheep"?

Could it be those outside of the holy Jewish huddle?

Or could it be those outside of *your* holy huddle?

After his death, Jesus comes alongside a couple of despondent followers who are walking away from Jerusalem on their way to the small town of Emmaus. They did not recognize this was Jesus who had joined them, as he asked them why they were so sad and what they were discussing so seriously. They rehearsed all of the happenings of the crucifixion and the reported resurrection with deep disappointment. Now get this! Their disappointment was narrowly focused on Abraham's Step 1. Luke records them saying, "But we were hoping that it was Jesus who was going to redeem Israel."

Hearing this, Jesus explains to them the mission of the Messiah by outlining Moses' teachings, the Prophets and the Psalms. Then, at dinner, when Jesus blessed and broke the bread, they recognized Jesus and he vanished.

They quickly returned to Jerusalem to tell the disciples what they had seen!

When gathered with the rest of the disciples, Jesus appeared among them. Then he opened their minds to understand the Scriptures and he said to them, "It is written that the Messiah would suffer and rise again from the dead on the third day, and that repentance for forgiveness of sins would be proclaimed in his name to *all the nations,* beginning from Jerusalem" (Luke 24).

All!

Can't be more inclusive than that!

How did we miss the point?

Jesus Commanded Abraham's 2-Step

After showing how to live out the 2nd Step of Abraham's covenant with God to be a blessing to the nations of the world and repeatedly teaching it everywhere he went, Jesus made it the primary mission for his early followers. He clearly directed them to follow through on this mission after his death. For years it's been referred to as the Great Commission.

First of all, the term "Great Commission" isn't even in the Bible! This title evolved to fire up the religious world to be givers and goers in order to convert the world to Christianity. So, going, baptizing, and converting the world became the mission of the "Great Commission," even though Jesus' command is simpler and clearer than that—*to make followers of Jesus in all the nations of the world!*

Note Jesus' words: "All authority in heaven and on earth has been given to me. Therefore, *make disciples of all nations*" (Matthew 28).

The late Dr. Ralph Winter, a world-famous expert in Christian missions around the world said, "Jesus didn't come to give the Great Commission; He came to take it back from the Jews who had it for 2000 years and done nothing with it." Why? Because they continually missed the point! Dr. Winter understood the "Great Commission" as introducing Jesus into the cultures of the world, not converting people out of those cultures into Western Christianity.

Then, after the resurrection and just before Jesus left, he directed his followers to wait in Jerusalem for the Spirit to come upon them: "But you will receive power when the Holy Spirit comes on you; and you will be my witnesses in Jerusalem, and in all Judea and Samaria, and *to the ends of the earth*" (Acts 1).

Jesus made it clear what he wanted his followers to do. They were to take the message of Jesus to the nations of the world. So, where is the narrow-minded exclusive Jesus in this?

Four Unblinkered Moments after the Resurrection

In Jerusalem. When the Spirit showed up in Jerusalem and came upon the disciples, "God-fearing Jews *from every nation under heaven*" were there (Acts 2).

In Samaria. The attractiveness of Jesus continued to increase. Philip took the message of Jesus to the Samaritan people, and the response was positive. The Samaritans "got it" (Acts 8).

Near Gaza. On a desert road near Gaza, Philip was sent for a divine appointment with an Ethiopian, a court official of Queen Candace of Ethiopia. The official was in charge of the Queen's treasure and was returning from worshiping God in Jerusalem. When he stopped his chariot to read from the Prophet Isaiah, Philip showed up right on time to answer the questions the Ethiopian was asking himself. They entered into a conversation about the identity of the servant that Isaiah described, and the Ethiopian was thrilled to understand the Good News of Jesus (Acts 8)!

At Caesarea. At the coastal city of Caesarea, Peter had one of the most interesting experiences a Jew could have! He was visiting a friend in the city of Joppa when he had a vision. At the same time in Caesarea there was a man named Cornelius, a centurion in what was known as the Italian Regiment (a non-Jew). He and all his family were devout and God-fearing; he gave generously to those in need and prayed to God regularly.

One day at about three in the afternoon he had a vision. He distinctly saw an angel of God, who came to him and said, "Cornelius!"

Cornelius stared at him in fear. "What is it, Lord?" he asked.

The angel answered, "Your prayers and gifts to the poor have come up as a memorial offering before God. Now send men to Joppa to bring back a man named Simon who is called Peter. He is staying with Simon the tanner, whose house is by the sea."

When the angel who spoke to him had gone, Cornelius called two of his servants and a devout soldier who was one of his attendants. He told them everything that had happened and sent them to Joppa.

About noon the following day as they were on their journey and approaching the city, Peter went up on the roof to pray. He became hungry and wanted something to eat, and while the meal was being prepared, he fell into a trance.

He saw heaven opened and something like a large sheet being let down to earth by its four corners. It contained all kinds of four-footed animals, as well as reptiles and birds.

Then a voice told him, "Get up, Peter. Kill and eat."

"Surely not, Lord!" Peter replied. "I have never eaten anything impure or unclean."

The voice spoke to him a second time, "Do not call anything impure that God has made clean."

This happened three times, and immediately the sheet was taken back to heaven.

While Peter was wondering about the meaning of the vision, the men sent by Cornelius found out where Simon's house was and stopped at the gate. They called out, asking if Simon who was known as Peter was staying there.

While Peter was still thinking about the vision, the Spirit said to him, "Simon, three men are looking for you. So get up and go downstairs. Do not hesitate to go with them, for I have sent them." Peter went down and said to the men, "I'm the one you're looking for. Why have you come?"

The men replied, "We have come from Cornelius the centurion. He is a righteous and God-fearing man, who is respected by all the Jewish people. A holy angel told him to ask you to come to his house so that he could hear what you have to say."

Then Peter invited the men into the house to be his guests.

The next day Peter started out with them, and some of the believers from Joppa went along. The following day he arrived in Caesarea. Cornelius was expecting them and had called together his relatives and close friends.

As Peter entered the house, Cornelius met him and fell at his feet in reverence. But Peter made him get up. "Stand up," he said, "I am only human myself."

Peter went inside and found a large gathering of people and said to them: "You are well aware that it is against our law for a Jew to associate with people from other nations (gentiles) or visit them. But God has shown me that I should not call anyone impure or unclean. So when I was sent for, I came without raising any objection. May I ask why you sent for me?"

Cornelius answered: "Three days ago I was in my house praying at this hour, at three in the afternoon. Suddenly a man in shining clothes stood before me and said, 'Cornelius, God has heard your prayer and remembered your gifts to the poor. Send to Joppa for Simon who is called Peter. He is a guest in the home of Simon the tanner, who lives by the sea.' So I sent for you immediately and it was good of you to come. Now we are all here in the presence of God to listen to everything the Lord has commanded you to tell us."

Then Peter began to speak: "I now realize how true it is that God does not show favoritism, but welcomes those *from every nation* who fear him and do what is right" (Acts 10).

Did you get that? God welcomes all who come, revering Him and doing what is right! Really, *all*?

Really.

Paul Lived Out Abraham's 2-Step

Here are a few examples in the life of Paul.

In Pisidian Antioch: Paul and his traveling partner, Barnabas, spoke in the synagogue in a place called Pisidian

Antioch. The response was so great that they were asked to return the next week. Nearly the whole city showed up to hear their words about Jesus. When the Jewish holy huddle saw the crowds, they were filled with jealousy. They began to contradict what Paul was saying and heaped abuse on him.

Then Paul and Barnabas answered them boldly: "We felt it was proper to speak the word of God to you first. Since you reject it and do not consider yourselves worthy of eternal life, we now turn to the nations of the world (gentiles) as was in God's original plan."

For this is what the Lord has commanded all of us: "I have made you a light for the nations, that you may bring salvation to the ends of the earth." They were quoting the prophet Isaiah, when he said: "It is too small a thing for you to be my servant to restore the tribes of Jacob and bring back those of Israel I have kept. I will also make you a light for the nations (gentiles), that my salvation may reach to the ends of the earth" (Isaiah 49).

When the non-Jews in the crowd heard this, they were glad! The word of the Lord spread through the whole region. But the Jewish leaders incited the God-fearing women of high standing and the leading men of the city so much that they stirred up persecution against Paul and Barnabas and expelled them from their region (Acts 13). All was very positive, until the Jews became jealous of God's inclusiveness.

In Athens: Paul spoke in the marketplace where lots of discussion and debate occurred. "People of Athens! I see that in every way you are very religious. For as I walked around and looked carefully at your objects of worship, I even found an altar with this inscription: TO AN UNKNOWN GOD. So you are ignorant of the very thing you worship— and this is what I am going to proclaim to you.

"The God who made *the world* and *everything in it*

is the Lord of heaven and earth and does not live in temples built by hands. And he is not served by human hands, as if he needed anything. Rather, he himself *gives everyone life and breath and everything else.* From one man he made *all the nations,* that they should inhabit *the whole earth;* and he marked out their appointed times in history and the boundaries of their lands. God did this so that they (*all nations and cultures*) would seek him and perhaps reach out for him and find him, though he is not far from any one of us. 'For in him we live and move and have our being.' As some of your own poets have said, 'We are his offspring.' Therefore since we are God's offspring, we should not think that the divine being is like gold or silver or stone—an image made by human design and skill" (Acts 17).

Paul, too, wants us all to see that God's message is to the whole world. God is already there, having marked out all cultures and nations. There is not one nation or one religious system that owns Jesus. Again, we have to ask ourselves. Where did we go wrong? Where did we miss the point?

In Jerusalem: Paul shared his story of being a persecutor of the followers of Jesus, then how he personally met Jesus. The crowd was with him up to this point, then all hell broke loose. Paul said: "And when the blood of Stephen was shed, I stood there giving my approval and guarding the clothes of those who were killing him.' but then the Lord said to me, 'Go; I will send you far away to the nations (Gentiles).' At these words about bringing the message to the nations, they raised their voices and shouted, "Rid the earth of him! He's not fit to live" (Acts 22)!

What happened? All was happy and comfortable.

Until Paul threatened to break up the huddle.

Paul before King Agrippa: Later on, a fascinating interaction between Paul and King Agrippa reveals the full truth

71

of the Abrahamic 2-Step and the violent reaction to it. "So then, King Agrippa, I was not disobedient to the vision from heaven. First to those in Damascus, then to those in Jerusalem and in all Judea, and then to the nations (gentiles), I proclaimed that they should change their minds and turn to God and demonstrate their changed hearts by their deeds. That is why some Jews seized me in the temple courts and tried to kill me.

"But God has helped me to this very day; so I stand here and continue to testify to small and great alike. I am saying nothing beyond what the prophets and Moses said would happen—that the Messiah would suffer and, as the first to rise from the dead, would bring the message of light to his own people *and to the nations*" (Acts 26).

Paul's letter to the Galatians: The followers of Jesus in Galatia were already beginning to form their own holy huddle. In Paul's letter to the followers of Jesus there he wrote, "Understand, then, that those who have faith are children of Abraham. Scripture foresaw that God would justify *the nations* by faith, and announced the 'good news' in advance to Abraham: 'All nations will be blessed through you.' So those who rely on faith are blessed along with Abraham, the man of faith.... He redeemed us in order that the blessing given to Abraham might come to *the nations* through Jesus, so that by faith we might receive the promise of the Spirit" (Galatians 3).

The Early Disciples Resisted Abraham's 2-Step

Maybe one of the most astounding facts of the early

Jesus movement is the resistance of the early leaders of the movement to be all-inclusive, even though God had made a special covenant with Abraham to bless the nations of the world. Moses taught this, the prophets taught this, Jesus taught this. And Jesus went so far as to command it of his followers: "Make disciples of all nations."

So who dropped the ball, and how?

The early leadership of the Jesus movement resisted it in two ways.

One: When people from the nations of the world wanted to follow Jesus, they were determined to make these non-Jewish followers Jews. They wanted to require circumcision! OUCH! After lots of discussions and arguments, this requirement was dismissed.

Two: The early leadership would not go outside of Jerusalem. They stayed right there and did not take the message of Jesus to the world. Why is this? Were they feeling their "power" and "positioning" and didn't want to lose it? Were they comfortable right where they were and didn't want to be inconvenienced? Did they think others would come to them?

It took an outbreak of persecution to push Jesus' followers outside of Jerusalem (Acts 8:1). It actually took an outright military siege of Jerusalem by the Roman general, Titus, in 70 A.D. to push them out of the city. Even then, James remained there, eventually becoming the Bishop of Jerusalem.

When Jesus' Followers Missed the Point— Big Time!

Missing the point and purpose of Jesus did not begin in the

organized religious institution as I have always thought. That's a myth! It began with the earliest followers of Jesus; even before the Jesus movement was officially launched! They missed it within a period of a few days (as recorded in Luke) in which they experienced the most miraculous adventure anyone could have ever imagined! There seems to be a natural tendency, no matter how much we have seen and heard, to become distracted away from the simplicity of Jesus plus nothing.

Luke records in the 9th chapter of his gospel account of the life of Jesus a most amazing few days in history. Get the progression of this short period of time and see how his early followers missed the point.

Jesus sends out his early followers on a miraculous field trip. Jesus empowered them to fight against evil, to cure diseases, to proclaim the message of the Kingdom and to heal the sick. What makes this most incredible is that Jesus sends out these disciples who aren't really believers yet nor do they yet believe Jesus is the Son of God. So they went out into many villages and performed their mission as prescribed by Jesus. Think of it! They are brand-new followers of Jesus and they have already been sent on a mission to perform incredible miracles! What an experience this must have been!

Next Jesus took them with him to a nearby fishing vilage in Galilee where great crowds followed them. After speaking to the crowds about the Kingdom of God and healing many of them, Jesus knew they needed to eat something, so he fed more than 5000 people with five loaves of bread and two fish. Jesus performed this spectacular miracle by using the "disciples" to distribute the food to the masses of people. What a thrill that must have been for these early followers!

Jesus then takes Peter, John, and James with him up on a mountain to pray. While praying, Jesus revealed his glory and brilliance as the visible presence of God right in front of them. Moses and Elijah supernaturally appear with them and then the voice of God pronounces Jesus as the Son of God. Again, this must have been an amazing experience for these three men.

When they came down from the mountain, a large crowd met them. A man was concerned for his son who was afflicted with seizures and convulsions and complained to Jesus that the other nine "disciples" were unable to heal him. Jesus moves into gear and heals this man's son right away. Everyone, including the "disciples," was amazed at this sight!

These early followers of Jesus have just returned from performing miracles in the villages, participating in the feeding of the 5000, three of them seeing Jesus in all his glory, and all seeing Jesus heal this desperate little boy. What a ride! What a miraculous adventure watching Jesus and actually working alongside him.

Now, note what happens in the next three scenes with the disciples. They so miss the point of Jesus and his message. An argument breaks out among the disciples: The argument? Which of them will be viewed as the greatest?

Jesus, knowing their thoughts, took a little child and had him stand beside him. Then he said to them, "Whoever welcomes this little child in my name welcomes me; and whoever welcomes me welcomes the one who sent me. For whoever is least among you all is the greatest." What's this all about? After all of this demonstration that Jesus is the pre-eminent One, they have already missed the point. Jesus is the point, not them or their comparative greatness!

Then the disciples become jealous over seeing another person doing things in the name of Jesus: John said, "Master, we saw someone driving out demons in your name and we tried to stop him, because he is not one of us."

"Do not stop him," Jesus said, "for whoever is not against you is for you."

Here we go! These early followers of Jesus are caught

up in setting up their own holy huddle! The problem is that there is a person doing things in the name of Jesus. Now note this! John says the problem with this person is that he is "not one of us." Do you get it? This guy who is doing terrific things in the name of Jesus just doesn't match up, because he is not a member of their little group. Ever heard or seen that attitude? Again, they are missing the point of Jesus. Their little group has become more important than Jesus, himself!

Then there is a problem with the response of the Samaritans. In another instance Jesus sent out a few of his followers to get things ready in Samaria. Jesus was planning to go through Samaria to teach and heal there. The Samaritans didn't welcome the preparation for Jesus, so James and John asked Jesus, "Lord, do you want us to call fire down from heaven to destroy them?" But Jesus turned and rebuked them.

See how it's getting worse! The disciples are now so miffed at the Samaritan's response that they are actually suggesting they must be destroyed. Note, it's more serious than this! They aren't asking Jesus to call down fire from heaven; they are thinking they might call the fire down to destroy the Samaritans! "Lord, do you want us to call fire down from heaven to destroy them?" Are you kidding me? These guys have not only missed the point and purpose of Jesus; *they* are taking on a little personal prominence for themselves.

There were three separate clashes over secondary matters. The 1st clash was between the disciples, the 2nd clash was between the disciples and other followers of Jesus, and then the 3rd clash is between the disciples of Jesus and a group of people from another religious system.

Who's the greatest? This guy is not one of us! Let's destroy these Samaritans who aren't receptive to our message!

All three clashes share three common characteristics: *Each clash* was motivated by the pride of being more "right" than another—all too common among those who claim to be followers of Jesus today.

Each clash was divisive. If you leave Jesus out of the equation of relationships within the kingdom, you will inevitably experience divisiveness.

Each clash was missing Jesus as the point of it all.

None of these responses was on-message with what these early followers have experienced in their walk with Jesus. They completely missed the point.

Here's the principle to keep in mind: *Jesus unites. Everything else divides.*

He is the point. And he *alone.*

Can I get personal for a moment?

Do *you* see it that way?

Or are you missing the point, too?

CHAPTER 5

How Did Jesus Plus Nothing Become Everything *But* Jesus?

How did Jesus plus nothing become everything *but* Jesus? And how does it keep happening today?

Jesus identified a primary flaw in the religious system as it was practiced. As he saw it, the flaw didn't reside within the people, but within the professionals. Jesus strongly criticized the religious leaders for their made-up commandments, meticulous rules, sacred traditions, and their man-made teachings that caused them to "set aside the commands of God."

There seem to be three tensions Jesus keeps at the forefront for those who want to follow him. These tensions were present in the 1st Century, they are present in the Western culture today, and they are present in a variety of ways throughout the cultures of the world.

To get a clearer picture of what was at the core of Jesus' teachings, let's unpack the three primary tensions to which Jesus referred. To do this, I want to use the words of Jesus.

Tension #1—Person vs. Program

This tension gets to the heart of living out Jesus plus nothing. It's the beginning of the process of missing the point of Jesus. It's the source of it all.

This could be more accurately described as "inner vs. outer." Jesus goes to the heart of the matter in his first seminar. The question in the air was: "Jesus, how does your teaching differ from what we've been taught?"

Right up front Jesus says, "Do not think that I have come to abolish the Law or the Prophets; I have not come to abolish them but to fulfill them. Truly I tell you, until heaven and earth disappear, not the smallest letter, not the least stroke of a pen, will by any means disappear from the Law until everything is accomplished.

"Anyone who sets aside one of the least of these commands and teaches others accordingly will be called least in the kingdom of heaven, but whoever practices and teaches these commands will be called great in the kingdom of heaven. For I tell you that unless your righteousness surpasses that of the Pharisees and the teachers of the law, you will certainly not enter the kingdom of heaven" (Matthew 5).

The Pharisees and the teachers of the law were extremely religious people and they showed off that religiosity to all who might see. Was Jesus suggesting that their righteousness (way of living) was not enough?

Yes!

Jesus wasn't pushing for more religious and super-spiritual shows in order to enter the Kingdom of heaven. Jesus was pushing to surpass the righteousness of the Pharisees by going internal. Instead of making your righteousness an external show, make it a matter of the heart!

To surpass the righteousness of the leaders of the day was to focus on the inner life (the internals) rather than the outer life (the externals).

Note Jesus' emphasis when the externalized Pharisees criticized him and his disciples for not washing their hands properly: "Are you still so dull? Don't you see that whatever enters the mouth goes into the stomach and then out of the body? But the things that come out of the mouth come from the heart, and these defile you. For out of the heart come evil thoughts, murder, adultery, sexual immorality, theft, false testimony, slander. These are what defile you; but eating with unwashed hands does not defile you"

(Matthew 15).

And another time Jesus says, "Woe to you, teachers of the law and Pharisees, you hypocrites! You clean the outside of the cup and dish, but inside they are full of greed and self-indulgence. Blind Pharisee! First clean the inside of the cup and dish, and then the outside also will be clean."

And later Jesus says, "Woe to you, teachers of the Law and Pharisees, you hypocrites! You are like whitewashed tombs, which look beautiful on the outside, but on the inside are full of the bones of the dead and everything unclean. In the same way, on the outside you appear to people as righteous but on the inside you are full of hypocrisy and wickedness" (Matthew 23).

The program of the religious leaders had a complicated, hierarchical system to it. When Jesus spoke of this, he said, "The teachers of the law and the Pharisees sit in Moses' seat. So you must be careful to do everything they tell you. But do not do what they do, for they do not practice what they preach. They tie up heavy, cumbersome loads and put them on other people's shoulders, but they themselves are not willing to lift a finger to move them. Everything they do is done for people to see: They make their phylacteries wide and the tassels on their garments long; they love the place of honor at banquets and the most important seats in the synagogues; they love to be greeted with respect in the marketplaces and to have people call them 'Rabbi.' But you are not to be called 'Rabbi,' for you have only one Master and you are all brothers. And do not call anyone on earth 'father,' for you have one Father, and he is in heaven. Nor are you to be called 'teacher,' for you have one Teacher, the Messiah. The greatest among you will be your servant. For those who exalt themselves will be humbled, and those who humble themselves will be exalted" (Matthew 23).

Person is about the internal over the external.

Program brings with it a system of externals in order to be seen "right."

Which is easier to follow?

It's much easier to follow a program with its lists of do's and don'ts. Just check it off the list, and before you know it, you're feeling pretty good about yourself. Maybe a little too good. This is not only deceptive to those looking on; it's deceptive to you if you think you are a little more "right" for following the program than others.

Maybe one of the most shocking dimensions of this process between *person* and *program* is found in Jesus' words about the Scriptures. There is no doubt in my mind that the biblical Scriptures teach Jesus throughout. When Jesus joined the two on their way to Emmaus, "beginning with Moses and all the Prophets, he explained to them what was said in all the Scriptures concerning himself" (Luke 24).

There seems to be a natural tendency to depersonalize the *person* of Jesus in Scriptures and endorse the *program* above the *person*. The result? Bibliolatry—the worship of the Scriptures! This is a subtle problem, but it is lethal. Bibliolatry is also taken another level to hold up one translation as "the official one," the one that has been stamped with some group's seal of approval. Many believe the King James is the closest version to the original you can get. The mantra is: "If it was good enough for Jesus, then it's good enough for us!" Never mind that it was written sixteen centuries after Jesus!

Jesus speaks directly to this after he is attacked for healing a man on Sabbath. Jesus says, "You study the Scriptures diligently because you think that in them you possess eternal life. These are the very Scriptures that testify about me, yet you refuse to come to me to have life" (John 5).

These religious leaders were diligent in following their program of study, yet missed the point of their study of the Scriptures.

The point?

Jesus.

At best, this first tension leaves Jesus on the sidelines; at worst, it leaves him behind. But regardless, the show must go on—the program must be promoted!

Tension #2—Relationship vs. Religion

This tension has to do with authentically following Jesus plus nothing. It is a relational lifestyle, not a religious one.

Jesus' revolutionary call, "follow me," is always within the context of a relationship. The real tension occurs when a person is invited into a relationship with Jesus, then is taught how to follow a religious system of do's and don'ts. Life will never come through a religious system, but only within a life-sustaining relationship with Jesus. These are not empty, ritualistic "God-words" to live by.

Don't miss this . . . The only way Jesus reveals himself or works with us is personally! Never impersonally as a Force or Energy . . . as an Idea or Cause . . . as a Fix or a Cure. This relational context with the person of Jesus is revolutionary! Even for Christians!

Note Jesus' context for teaching. He seemed to do his best work around a table—tabletop fellowship, discussing while eating and drinking.

Jesus' encounter with Matthew. A good example of the revolutionary call combined with tabletop fellowship is when Jesus extended his revolutionary call to Matthew: As Jesus went on from there, he saw a man named Matthew sitting at the tax collector's booth. "Follow me," he said, and Matthew got up and followed him.

The revolutionary call—"follow me"—is all about relationship, not religion. Jesus never says, "follow a set of rules." It's "follow me!" It's not, "get your act together and follow me!" It's not, "become religious and follow me!" It's not, "do something to earn God's acceptance and follow me!'

In the case of Matthew—a despised tax-collector, a

traitor to his people to work for the Romans, a non-religious loser, who never made the grade to follow a rabbi as a kid—now Jesus, the most popular new rabbi on the scene approaches Matthew with an air of "I accept you as you are, now follow me!"

No doubt Matthew had been exposed to Jesus' teachings along the seashore and was attracted to him as so many were. Now, to be personally approached by Jesus, it was mind-boggling to him! He must have felt the love and acceptance, because he quickly responded. He must have called his family and friends right away and invited them all to his house to celebrate.

While Jesus was having dinner at Matthew's party, many tax collectors and sinners came and ate with him and his disciples. When the Pharisees saw this, they asked his disciples, "why does your teacher eat with tax collectors and sinners?" This is the best thing about tabletop fellowship in a private home. You get to meet many of the family and friends in the process. Matthew's friends were other tax collectors and sinners (the non-religious). When the religious saw this, they began to grumble.

This sets up two of the most amazing teachings of Jesus. On hearing this, he said, "it is not the healthy who need a doctor, but the sick." He first makes it clear that he came to call the sinners, the non-religious, the spiritually disenfranchised, into relationship and not the righteous.

Jesus goes on to clarify this with a fascinating statement: "but go and learn what this means: 'I desire mercy, not sacrifice.' For I have not come to call the righteous, but sinners" (Matthew 9).

Wasn't it God who set up the elaborate sacrificial system for the Jews to follow? Yet it was God who first said this through the ancient prophet, Hosea: "I desire mercy (a heart of compassion), not sacrifice, and acknowledgement of God rather than burnt offerings" (Hosea 6). Jesus quoted these words from Hosea and solved the tension between *relationship* and *religion*. Relationship gets God's vote every time! In His eyes, mercy is better than sacrifice, and knowledge of Him is better than burnt offerings.

This is Good News to those who are religiously out of it, under the guilt pile, or behind in their religious duties, and annoying news to those who have performed the sacrificial system flawlessly.

Note the content of Jesus' further teachings on this tension. On three occasions Jesus specifically moves his listeners from religion to relationship.

Jesus' encounter with the crowds after feeding the 5000. They were obviously impressed with the Jesus "special meal" that he had just provided. But within the meal was a message. Jesus urged them to trust him and his teachings. Just as they ate the fish and bread, now Jesus urges them to receive him as the bread of life that will satisfy their deepest hunger. So they asked him, "what sign then will you give that we may see it and believe you? What will you do? Our ancestors ate the manna in the wilderness; as it is written: 'He gave them bread from heaven to eat.'"

Jesus said to them, "very truly I tell you, it is not Moses who has given you the bread from heaven, but it is my Father who gives you the true bread from heaven. For the bread of God is the bread that comes down from heaven and gives life to the world."

"Sir," they said, "always give us this bread."

Then Jesus declared, "I am the bread of life. whoever comes to me will never go hungry, and whoever believes in me will never be thirsty."

At this the Jews there began to grumble about him because he said, "I am the bread that came down from heaven" (John 6).

They were so resistant to accepting Jesus as being sent by God, they tried to turn the conversation to their religious history and theology. Jesus' response? "I am the new manna in town!"

It's not a program from Moses.

It's not part of their religious history.

This is personal!

This is relational!

Then there's Jesus' encounter with Mary and Martha at their brother's death . . . Jesus' very good friend, Lazarus, died and Jesus showed up four days late. Lazarus' two sisters were exasperated that Jesus didn't come earlier. Mary and Martha both said to Jesus, "Lord, if you had been here, our brother would not have died."

While speaking with Martha, Jesus said, "Your bother will rise again." Immediately Martha moved into her theological system by saying, "I know he will rise again in the resurrection at the last day." Jesus quickly corrects her by saying, "*I* am the resurrection and the life. Anyone who believes *in me* will live, even though he dies" (John 11).

Again, Jesus makes it personal!

Finally, there's Jesus' encounter with his early followers before his death . . . while with his disciples the last week of his life, he tells them he is going to die and come back, speaking of the resurrection. Then he says, "you know the way to the place where I am going." Thomas said to him, "Lord, we don't know where you are going, so how can we know the way?"

Here we go again! Thomas is looking for a set of directions, a program to follow, a system to obey.

Jesus responds to this with a relational response: "I am the way and the truth and the life."

This isn't about a set of directions.

This isn't religious.

It's personal!

Tension #3—Majors vs. Minors

This tension seems to be concerned with the emphasis we place on what's important. For those who follow after *program* rather than the *person*, for those who follow after *religion* rather than *relationship*, there is a tendency to struggle with what's most important. It's a tendency to *major in the minors* and minor in the majors.

The religious leaders in the 1st Century were some of the most religious people ever. Their religiosity was all about external matters—separation from sin and sinners and cleansing oneself. They were known . . . . for professing righteousness without possessing it, for being hyper-critical hair-splitters, theological nit-pickers, and for emphasizing the letter of the Law over the spirit of the Law—all truth and little grace, and making absolutes out of non-absolutes—lists and lists of rules and regulations!

These hyper-critical, super-spiritual people are still around today. In fact, I saw one with a bullhorn outside a Dalai Lama gathering, condemning all who were attending, informing us that we were all going to hell!

Because of their diligence in majoring in the minors and minoring in the majors, the Pharisees delighted in pointing out where Jesus' followers kept coming up short. Here's an illustration: the Pharisees and some of the teachers of the law who had come from Jerusalem gathered around Jesus and saw some of his disciples eating food with hands that were defiled, that is, unwashed (the Pharisees and all the Jews do not eat, unless they give their hands a ceremonial washing, holding to the tradition of the elders. When they come from the marketplace they do not eat unless they wash. And they observe many other traditions, such as the washing of cups, pitchers, and kettles).

So the Pharisees and teachers of the Law asked Jesus, "Why don't your disciples live according to the tradition of the elders, instead of eating their food with defiled hands?"

He replied, "Isaiah was right when he prophesied about you hypocrites; as it is written: 'These people honor me with their lips, but their hearts are far from me. They worship me in vain; their teachings are merely human rules.' You have let go of the commands of God and are holding on to human traditions." And he continued, "You have a fine way of setting aside the commands of God in order to observe your own traditions . . . . Thus you nullify the word of God by your tradition that you have handed down. And you do many things like that" (Mark 7).

Later, Jesus rails against these religious hypocrites, when he says, "Woe to you, teachers of the law and Pharisees, you hypocrites! You give a tenth of your spices—mint, dill, and cumin. But you have neglected the more important matters of the law—justice, mercy, and faithfulness. You should have practiced the latter, without neglecting the former. You blind guides! You strain out a gnat but swallow a camel" (Matthew 23).

Jesus was most concerned with these tensions in the 1st Century. These were serious problems then and now! These tensions are at the core of what gets in the way of Jesus plus nothing. They deflect and distract us away from the simplicity of following Jesus.

These tensions end up becoming list after list of add-ons. I think it begins with the religious professionals. Over the years they wanted to show how much more knowledgeable they are by inventing more and more ideas, concepts, rules, and sacraments that they claim to be core to the basic religious belief system. It's what scientists and educators do to prove their credentials. They are driven to complicate things rather than to simplify them. They earn their credentials by being the ones who claim to understand all of the complexities—things we mere mortals could never really grasp on our own.

Here's more of how Jesus scolds the religious leaders for their many add-ons that seem to be more caught than taught as these leaders set the example: Then Jesus said to the crowds and to his disciples: "Woe to you, teachers of the law and Pharisees, you hypocrites! You shut the door of the kingdom of heaven in people's faces. You yourselves do not enter, nor will you let those enter who are trying to. Woe to you, teachers of the law and Pharisees, you hypocrites! You travel over land and sea to win a single convert, and then you make that convert twice as much a child of hell as you are" (Matthew 23).

Jesus was warning them that their religious expression had become buried under piles and piles of add-ons. When I first seriously studied Jesus' words here, I began to see how my religious expression of Christianity had been buried in a myriad of layers that produced a man-made effect.

For instance, I grew up as a Baptist. All of our particular brand of Baptist believed and practiced the same things. No dancing! No movies! No drinking! No smoking! No nothing! Now you might think this is close to Jesus plus nothing, but it wasn't. Instead of Jesus plus nothing, it was Baptists plus nothing. Jesus was quite incidental to the lifestyle we were taught to live.

We were all afraid. Afraid of the possibility of going to hell. Afraid of God's judgment on our lives. Afraid of anyone knowing our brokenness—*truly* knowing us. Afraid of being caught sinning. Afraid of Jesus returning. Afraid of being left behind when he did return.

We weren't a cult, but we were caught up in what I call the "culting" process! We were buried under the many layers of cultural traditions, man-made commandments, social causes and concerns. The culting process is based upon the desire to be "right," at least, more right than others around me. These layers of add-ons succeeded in producing a counterfeit of the real thing.

We had a "Church Covenant" on the right wall of the church. As a kid, I stared at it often. There were 10 things on the list that we couldn't do, if you wanted to go to heaven. And I did! But I found this to be depressing, because as I contemplated them, I realized 7 of the 10 were my goals in life!

Three Agendas

The culting process is all about *control, short-cuts*, and *reformation.*

Control is a common problem among humans. Most cultures of the world have a "garden" story where life begins. The garden is where the Creator-God sets the rules of life. In the Adam-and-Eve garden story their response was basically, "Thanks for the advice, but we'll be doing this our way!"

Aaron, Moses' associate pastor, so to speak, became impatient with Moses for not returning soon enough from his meeting with God. So, Aaron gathered all of the people's jewelry to melt it down to make a calf—a golden calf that would serve as a tangible, touchable god for the people. This was a form of control—forming a god you can see, touch, and visit whenever you want.

Throughout history using the agenda of control was prevalent. Do you think Constantine had any other agenda than control? The Crusades were all about control. The threat of religious persecution operates under the agenda of control. The fear of hell always seems to work best to control the people.

Short cuts to God present themselves as an attractive agenda. Everyone wants to know for sure they have done or are doing what's necessary to get their ticket to get into heaven. Membership, confirmation, baptism, a clean life, volunteer service, and financial contributions are just a few of the things on the punch card.

In my world it was going forward at an altar call, so at one point I counted about 36 times I went to the altar (42, if I count youth camp). But nothing ever changed. Somehow it never made that much difference.

Short cuts become problematic. When you think you have your pass or ticket, you tend to condemn others who didn't come to God in the same way. They just aren't going to make it. They're not one of us, so they are out of luck. This is the blinkered thinking of the last chapter . . . rigid, dogmatic, and narrow-minded.

Reformation is the third agenda of the culting process. Reformation feeds on the first two agenda dynamics—control and short cuts. Reformation's agenda is to change behavior and therefore control these behaviors. Reformation's agenda searches for short cuts to make the behavioral changes easier.

Reformation can only change the outside—fit you into a behavioral mold. It never goes far enough. Reformation is a little like straightening deck chairs on the Titanic. The deck looks better, but the boat is still going to sink. What is desperately needed is transformation—from the inside out.

The culting process is alive and well today as it was in the 1st century. Keep the people under control. Search for the short cuts that short-circuit the process of life's journey. Find a way to get that ticket into heaven and look on others with pity. Don't seek to be transformed. Seek to get others to reform their ways and come along with the herd—your particular herd is best!

The Jewish law had 248 commandments and 365 prohibitions. That's 613 laws to keep! Do you see how easy it is to pick and choose what's most important to you?

Most every religious system has a similar list—some more, some less! It's no wonder religion has been so divisive throughout history. But what if we determined to major in the majors and minor in the minors? This is Jesus' point throughout his teachings.

Major in the *person* of God; minor in the *program*.

Major in the *relationship* with God; minor in the *religion*.

91

The culting process doesn't have a chance if we make the main thing the main thing!

CHAPTER 6

How Can You Expect to Reach the World for God without God First Reaching Your Heart?

When I was on the faculty of Dallas Theological Seminary, I was the speaker at a weekend retreat where we had a Q & A session. I was asked a question by a prominent board member of the seminary that I answered by saying, "That's a very good question. I don't know, but I'll get back to you on that."

On Tuesday I was called into a meeting with our department chairman. He referenced the weekend and the question. He said, "Why did you say 'I don't know' when answering Dr. Smith's question?"

I said, "I answered it that way, because I didn't know."

He leaned across the desk toward me with his very long, outstretched index finger and said, "a Dallas man knows!" It was then that I realized that when there is no room for honest doubts and questioning what is the truth, there is little room for being a constant learner of the truth.

Even though I disagreed with this thinking, I still was marked by it in such a way that I set out to always have an answer. I quietly worked my way through many of my doubts, but I did it all alone. Therefore, I avoided several of the deeper, honest doubts like the plague. I set out to know and to communicate what I knew better than anyone else.

I have found doubts become more and more troublesome when they are not faced. They even seem to compound themselves over time. And, when you are Senior Pastor of a mega-Church, having spoken and published extensively, you are set up as one who knows. Then people count on you and look to you for answers to their questions. When you find yourself playing the role as the "Bible Answer Man" and yet have real gnawing doubts about your answers, a painful emptiness begins to fill up your own soul.

As I observed and continued to experience the religious, culting process, I was hurled into a pile of doubts, which I will soon share with you. I was expected to have the answers, yet I knew in my gut that I didn't. Doubts aren't bad; they are natural and everyone has them. In many ways, it's like anger. Anger is also normal and universal. Anger is not good or bad, right or wrong; what makes it good or bad is how you handle it. Anger must be processed and not allowed to fester into bitterness. The same is true of doubts. Doubts must be faced and not allowed to linger. If you don't discipline yourself to face your doubts, you end up trying to live your life the best way you can. I ended up living life *my way* for God, which in the end didn't work.

Honest Doubts

Doubt lingers somewhere between belief and disbelief. It entails a sense of uncertainty and even distrust of a perceived fact or reality. Doubt tends to place you in the state of inaction, maybe rendering you paralyzed to some degree.

Most of my time ministering as a conference speaker, a counselor and as Pastor, my own personal doubts were compounded for two reasons. First, I was too busy to take the time to think. No matter your philosophy of ministry, the religious organization can suck you dry with meetings and decisions and paying attention to the people—especially the "right" people. Second, I spent more time than the average pastor in the counseling room with thousands of people. Being the answer to their questions and needs was my addiction—my drug of choice. I had a messianic addiction to be all things to all people. Internally, it was sick and wrong and nearly killed me. Externally, it made me more loved and appreciated.

The Doubts I Accumulated

Can we talk? I mean *really* talk? Honestly. Openly. Without fear of reprimand or rejection. I want to share some things with you that I think are common to everyone who is trying to live out their faith honestly. Here are a few of the honest doubts that kept pestering me and causing a low-grade depression of sorts. I have grouped them into five categories, which are not exhaustive, merely representative:

Doubt One—Existence of God

Does God really exist or is He a creation of man? Is it possible to have a relationship with God? Why is He so hidden and difficult to find? Where is God when awful things happen to good people? Where is He when it hurts? I know these doubts sound basic, but when you are supposed to know *without a doubt* in order to be dogmatic enough to lead people, a gnawing sensation does occur.

Doubt Two—Exclusivity

Are Christians really the only ones who will get into heaven? Is Christianity the only way to heaven and all others are destined to hell? Will a loving, all-powerful God send people to hell who weren't born into the Christian culture or who never heard the truth about him? Is God really waiting and counting on Christians to convert the rest of the world to Christianity?

Doubt Three—Authority

Is the Bible true? How do we know? Who is able to accurately interpret the Bible? From time to time there were Bible verses that just didn't seem to say what the pastor taught, however I learned to go along with the crowd at a very early age. To deny the pastor's authority was unthinkable! I found, once you get into the groove of going along with your spiritual crowd, you build on these shared beliefs and look for others who believe as you do. The tendency is to build layer after layer of things that only agree with your belief. I grew up with the sense of blindly accepting the word of the pastor without question, and then I became the pastor making my own pronouncements and interpretations.

Doubt Four—The Second Coming of Jesus

Is Jesus really coming back? Hasn't the second coming of Jesus always been taught throughout the ages? Why has he not shown up yet? Why do others seem to know when Jesus will return, when Jesus himself says that he doesn't even know? Will I be taken when Jesus comes back or left behind?

Doubt Five—Conversion Tactics of Christian Evangelism

I grew up being taught that Jesus wanted the entire world to be converted to Christianity; I was taught my responsibility before God was to make everyone in my reach a Christian. Actually, my Baptist upbringing was narrower than that. They not only believed Jesus wanted the world to be Christian, but Baptist. Is this really what Jesus intended? If so, Jesus wasn't talking about it! At least, I never saw this in the Bible.

Here Is Where I Really Missed the Point

I had ears to hear, but I was listening to the wrong voices: seminary profs, spiritual gurus, popular writers, psychological and sociological experts, and others I wanted to please and impress.

I was listening to everyone . . . but Jesus!

I had eyes to see, but I was looking in the wrong

things: I studied the best research, learned the best practices, read the best books, followed the best advice.

I was watching everything . . . but Jesus!

In other words, I spent so much of my life filling my mind with things that just didn't matter. All I heard and all I saw were concepts and doctrines, principles and precepts, best practices and impressive outlines, humorous illustrations and memorable big ideas. These were all great and even powerful in a human sort of way. People did seek after God and found some life answers through it all.

What I was missing were ears to hear Jesus and eyes to see him. I knew a lot about Jesus, reached out to thousands with his amazing teachings, but I had never allowed Jesus to reach me.

After my kingdom crashed and burned with my resignation from the mega-Church, a painful divorce, and the obligatory trashing of a fallen leader, I caught a glimpse of Jesus as the only person who could possibly recycle my failure into something of worth. I regrouped a bit and thought I could start over, yet in my well-intentioned restart I became caught up in a new form of the same old religious programming, leaving Jesus behind again. And again, it didn't work.

But I Was Busy Reaching the World

My restart wasn't working. I was too busy to get to know Jesus, to *really* get to know him. I was speaking on his teachings I learned in the past, but I was too busy to meditate on his teachings in the present. I was counseling others on "What Would Jesus Do?" but I was too busy to stop and listen to what he wanted *me* to do. I was truly working for Jesus, but more in an advisory capacity.

Although I was good at criticizing the religious leaders of Jesus' day, I had slipped into their hypocritical lifestyle in a subtle way. I always taught other leaders to be careful not to become who they were preaching against. The religious leaders who rant against prostitutes and porn are frequently found with a prostitute and a porn addiction. Those who loudly and hatefully blast the homosexual community have been exposed as having homosexual encounters themselves.

I hated with a passion modern day Pharisaism and the super-spiritual, yet I became guilty of the same things. Again, I had ears to hear, but was not hearing. I had eyes to see, but I was not seeing. I was missing the point. I was missing Jesus.

I was so into reaching the world that I became blinded by my own efforts, however passionate, however well-meaning. My entire life I had been missing the point. I desperately needed Jesus to reach me. Instead of "out-reach," I needed "in-reach." Instead of me reaching the world, I needed him to reach my heart.

According to Jesus, all spiritual growth begins on the inside.

- "Clean the inside of the cup and dish first, then the outside will be clean."

- "First take the log out of your own eye, and then you will see clearly to remove the speck from the other person's eye."

- "Let anyone who is thirsty come to me and drink. Whoever believes in me, as Scripture has said, rivers of living water will flow from within them."

This emphasis on the internals is embodied in Jesus and his teachings. On many instances the response to Jesus' teachings is utter amazement. They were amazed that he taught as one who had authority in himself and not as their teachers who had to quote someone else for authority.

Inner transformation of a person's heart is required

before reaching out to others. When my wife and I embarked on this journey of following Jesus, we had no idea it was this inner transformation that we were seeking. Diana earnestly prayed that Jesus would create in her a new heart. She didn't want a bypass; she wanted a transplant. Me, I was tired of just talking about Jesus; I longed to *really* know, *really* follow him.

With our hearts bent toward Jesus, open to whatever he wanted from us, open to wherever he wanted us to go, and open to however he wanted us to live, we abandoned our former lifestyle in order to follow after him.

We dismantled a small church we were leading, shut down my professional speaking gigs, gathered a few friends to come along with us, and learned to be in the Jesus mode of attraction and not promotion.

We wanted Jesus to transform our hearts more than anything else. We wanted to know we could relate to Jesus in a personal, day-to-day manner. We wanted to learn to wait on Jesus to lead out with orders and opportunities. We wanted to experience what it means to ruthlessly trust Jesus.

Once Jesus had our hearts, he clearly made himself known to us. We prayed to know Jesus, longed for him, yet we were still shocked when he began to show up.

Missing the point of knowing and following Jesus without religious baggage came to a screeching halt, when Jesus apprehended our hearts.

I often think of how I used to say to audiences who knew what to do but didn't do it. I said, "when I passed out the pipe for you all to smoke, some of you didn't inhale!" This is precisely what happened to me. I put the pipe up to my mouth on several occasions in my life, but never inhaled . . . until now!

Part II

the pre-eminence of

Jesus

CHAPTER 7

Was Jesus a Christian?

Whether you see Jesus as a great man, guru, teacher, prophet, or simply a higher power, there is no doubt that he stands in a pre-eminent position throughout history. Now, remember, I'm not talking religion or a religious system. I'm not even speaking about Christianity. I am referring to Jesus alone, *simply* Jesus.

The question I want you to consider is: was Jesus a Christian?

My contention is: He *wasn't*.

To identify Jesus as a Christian is to limit him to the Western culture, to deny his Middle Eastern roots, and to prevent him from being embraced by the rest of the world.

The belief that Jesus was a Christian is a myth, and a deadly one at that. History has proven this over and over. Let's examine a few foundational myths about Jesus and Christianity.

First Myth—Jesus Is Owned by Christianity

Now don't get nervous about this. There is nothing wrong with being a Christian or belonging to Christianity. I want to help you consider a very basic understanding that causes lots of misunderstanding both in this country and in nations around the world.

Christian is not a common biblical term. In fact, only two writers of the Bible ever mentioned it—Luke, twice, and Peter, once. Jesus, Matthew, Mark, John, Paul, James, and Jude never mentioned it. Most people assert that Jesus was a Christian. Most would agree that Jesus would be comfortable being called a Christian and identifying himself exclusively with Christianity. But it is a myth. And the collateral damage from this myth has been devastating.

Many Christians believe they have a corner on the market with respect to Jesus. The by-product of believing Jesus is owned by Christianity is an ugly, religious pride. This pride leads Christians to identify their culture as the right culture—the "right" way of life. The Jews were the chosen people of God. Christians believe that they are the chosen people of God today. Because of this belief, this excludes all other cultures God created. But Christians have their answer: all others must convert to become Christians!

If you desire to become a follower of Jesus, this misconception will distract you and others away from him. Instead of following Jesus, the focus can so easily shift to becoming a Christian, defending Christianity, and setting one on a mission of converting others to become Christians. All of this distraction leaves Jesus behind.

Most non-Christians believe Jesus is exclusively related to Christians, and therefore they have no possible relationship with him, even though Jesus is so attractive, irresistible, and relevant to them.

Most non-Christians identify Jesus with the disastrous and horrendous actions of the Christian past and present— the Crusades against the Muslims and the persecution and killings of the Jews—all in the name of Christianity. The collateral damage is that Jesus becomes guilty by association.

Most non-Christians identify Christianity with the West, and as they develop hate for the West, they develop hate for Christianity (and vice versa). When Christians attempt to convert people who are not Christians, they stir up such anger and hate—especially in the non-Christian cultures. Christians want Hindus, Buddhists, Jews, Muslims, and whoever else to become Christians—to be converted away from their cultures into Western Christianity.

This aggressive approach was never the way of Jesus.

I see three ways to debunk this popular myth:

First, Jesus never used the term "Christian." The term is found three times in the New Testament. The first occurrence is in Acts 11:26: "and when he found him, he brought him to Antioch. So for a whole year Barnabas and Saul met with the church and taught great numbers of people. The disciples were called Christians first at Antioch."

The second occurrence is in Acts 26:28: "Then Agrippa said to Paul, 'Do you think that in such a short time you can persuade me to be a Christian?'"

The third time the term "Christian" is used is in 1 Peter 4:16: "However, if you suffer as a Christian, do not be ashamed, but praise God that you bear that name."

When I use the argument that Jesus never used the term "Christian," I am saying that he had something so different in mind than to offer a label to be worn or an organization to join—all to be foisted upon the cultures of the world. If Jesus were trying to change people's cultural identification, he would have actually done so. *But he didn't!*

Not only is the term "Christian" rarely mentioned, we know it is a man-made term. At first, Christian was used as one of the many tags placed on the followers of Jesus. It was never intended as a serious organizational label. "People of the Way" and "Nazarenes" were also popular identifications. Emperor Constantine chose a group of bishops to meet in 325 A.D. for the purpose of establishing a creed for the new religion that would be the basis for his political kingdom. He didn't do this for religious reasons; he did it for political reasons. So the bishops settled on the formation of the Christian Church. It was out of this meeting that the early creeds of Christianity were written. This was the official launch of Christianity.

Second, Jesus had a better term. Most Christians love to use the ID, "believer" or "born again." What's interesting is that with a couple of exceptions "believer," "believe," and "born again" are used only by John in his Gospel. John and all of the other Gospel writers—Matthew, Mark, and Luke—do use the same and most prominent terminology as they quote Jesus. All four Gospels are in agreement about the terms "follower" or "follow." This is Jesus' designation of those who are in relationship with him—followers.

Third, there is nothing wrong with being a Christian or even a Western Christian, if that's your cultural background. But there is something far better, and that is to be a follower of Jesus. The largest spiritual movements in the world are happening among Animists in Africa, Buddhists and Hindus in Asia, Muslims and Jews in the Middle East and around the world, atheists and agnostics in China and even Christians in the United States. This movement numbers in the millions. Other than those within the Western Christian cultural context, this movement consists of those who do not identify themselves with Christianity or Western Christianity, but all sincerely and enthusiastically call themselves followers of Jesus.

All have come to love and even worship Jesus!

How can this be? Because Jesus is more pre-eminent than we have let him be. Jesus doesn't fit into any religious box. He is the most attractive, the most irresistible, and the most relevant.

Second Myth—Jesus Is the Founder of Christianity

This myth may be one of the most difficult for all cultures to accept as a myth, but hear me out. Open up your hearts and minds and let's examine why I call this a myth. Remember, we're trying to understand the teachings and principles of Jesus, not the teachings and principles of our religious instruction and backgrounds. If I were to hold on to my background understandings, I would still believe Jesus was a Baptist!

Most people throughout the world believe that Jesus founded Christianity and the Christian Church. Earlier I referenced the political act of Constantine that officially established the Christian Church and its creeds. Even though this is a fact, many still assume that Jesus' intent and purpose was to found the religious system of Christianity as God's home on earth and to establish the organized Church as God's way of changing the world.

Jesus did say "I will build my church," but his idea of the church was an organism, not an institution; a movement, not an establishment; a gathering of followers, not a gathering of creeds, relics, and property. The organized Church provides lots of services for the consumer, but it wasn't what Jesus intended. In Jesus' time there already was an organized church in existence—the synagogue. He didn't speak against it, but only against its leadership.

The damage of believing the myth that Jesus founded Christianity or the organized Christian Church is threefold.

First, the religion of Christianity tends to become a substitute for the personal relationship with Jesus. Jesus commonly is left out of the Christian, religious, expression of faith. One of my hobbies is to read over Christian newsletters and articles to see if Jesus made the editorial cut. It is amazing how many times he is left out. Just recently a major article was published in a secular magazine about a visible and prominent Christian leader and his plan to change the world. Sadly, Jesus never made it into any part of the plan, nor did he even receive an honorable mention.

Second, the organized Christian Church tends to become a substitute for a personal relationship with Jesus and with his people. This produces spectators and not participators. It's just too easy to check off church attendance as one of the things you feel you must do. But as powerful as the church experience might be through authentic worship and exceptional messages, the once-a-week "show" just isn't what Jesus intended. The Jews already had this experience in the Synagogue. There's nothing wrong with it. Jesus had a better idea!

Third, when you believe Jesus is the founder of Christianity or the organized Christian Church, you expect him to be the architect of what is done in the name of Christianity and by the local organized Christian Church. The result of this thinking? Jesus gets the blame for whatever goes wrong. He gets tied to the moral failures of pastors. He gets tied to the endless fundraisers, the misappropriation of funds, the lavish lifestyles, the excessive expenditures.

Jesus was a founder.

But not of the Church as we know it.

And not of Christianity as we know it.

To link Jesus with the organized Church or with the religious system of Christianity caricaturizes Jesus beyond recognition. The world then criticizes Jesus and his movement on earth based upon the Church and upon the religious system.

To believe this second myth limits Jesus in almost every way. He is pre-eminent above all things, peoples, and religious systems. To keep Jesus in the position of being the founder of Christianity keeps him in an exclusive box, unavailable to the rest of the world.

Jesus nor any of his disciples bashed the Synagogue of the day, which equates to the Church today. There was no movement to plant new synagogues (churches) to compete with the primary synagogue in the city.

Therefore, *the dynamic, relational movement Jesus launched was not about building an organization or a monument; he set in motion a movement that was loosely held together.* This movement was not to take the place of the synagogue, nor is it to take the place of the organized (big C) Church today. The Jesus movement takes priority over any organization or religious system.

It was to be a movement that orbited around and

within the synagogue (church), the community, and the marketplace, demonstrating the love of Jesus to all. This movement doesn't have the privilege of gathering spectators together, because its all about participation in a fellowship, learning to love God and love one another. I call this movement the church of Jesus with a little c—the gathering of the followers of Jesus into a fellowship. It's a place to learn how to share, live life, and practice the principles and teachings of Jesus.

Big C Church was not taught nor was it in his mind or in the practice of the early disciples as they spread the message of Jesus and the Kingdom. In fact, the term "church" was not a major theme for Jesus. Jesus uses the term "church" only three times, because his primary teaching was the Good News of the Kingdom.

The book of Acts is sometimes called the *Acts of the Apostles,* but I think it's best to refer to it as the *Acts of Jesus.* And he hasn't stopped acting since. The purpose of the movement is to do one of the most difficult things ever—introducing Jesus to the world by demonstrating him to the world—by walking, talking, thinking, and loving like Jesus. You see, Jesus doesn't want you to demonstrate *for* him, but to be a demonstration *of* him—of his love and his peace.

Jesus launched a revolutionary movement. Are you participating in this movement—the orbiting (little c) church movement Jesus founded—or are you still a spectator in a big C Church? You can do both and gain much out of your experience, but don't miss out on making the Jesus movement your priority in your community right where you live. Jesus is already moving in the world around you. He's looking for you to join him there.

The Jesus movement that orbits around the organized Church and the community is not made up of only Christians. The make-up of the Jesus movement is a vast variety of people from all kinds of cultural backgrounds. What holds this movement together is that each person, no matter his or her religious background, is a follower of Jesus.

Third Myth—Jesus Is Narrow and Exclusive

In Jesus' first seminar in Matthew 5-7, he made a radical statement with respect to his relationship with the Jewish Law and traditions. He said, "Do not think that I have come to abolish the Law or the Prophets; I have not come to abolish them but to fulfill them."

Literally, Jesus didn't come to abolish the laws and traditions of the Jewish culture; he came to fulfill them. The Jewish culture, with its Law and traditions, was like a glass container, so to speak. Jesus came to fill that glass to the brim. He came to bring ultimate meaning and fullness to the Jewish religious system. Jesus is the way, the truth, and the life for all the Jewish dreams and yearnings. In the same way, I believe that he is the way, the truth, and the life for all cultural and religious systems and traditions. He is the meaning and fullness everyone is looking for. He fills up the various glasses of every culture.

This may seem a little far-fetched for you to embrace at first, but give it some thought. We are finding the footprints of Jesus in every culture. Years ago Don Richardson wrote a groundbreaking book *Eternity in Their Hearts.* He demonstrated that the fingerprints of the Creator-God was found to be in many cultures. God is already there, because God placed "eternity in their hearts."

In the movie, *Fingerprints of God in Japan,* the Creator-God of the Japanese people is clearly revealed. In the past (and still happening today in some places) the Japanese people were told they had to reject their Japanese roots and culture in order to be converted to Western Christianity. However, it is now clear that the Creator-God of the Japanese people was known to be in the form of a tri-unity or Godhead. Their Creator-God had a Japanese name, *"Ameno-mi-nakanushi,"* not the Jewish name,

Jehovah. When the Japanese watch this film, they weep with great joy. They don't have to reject their culture or feel they are an after-thought of God; God created them and is already present there.

This same understanding has happened among the Hawaiians and Polynesians, Buddhists, Hindus and Chinese. What's interesting is that in many of these cultures there are similar stories—the flood, sacrifices for sins, and many have a garden scene. In several of these cultures their ancient scriptures speak of a sacrifice for their sins that must be made by God Himself.

Where did these stories come from?

These are the fingerprints of God in the many cultures of the world.

Anyone in any culture or on any continent can be a follower of Jesus—cultural Jews, Hindus, Buddhists, Animists, Agnostics, Moslems, and Christians can all be followers of Jesus. Christians have said for years that a cultural Jew doesn't have to renounce being Jewish in order to follow Jesus. Following Jesus can make a person's Jewishness more full and meaningful. I believe this translates into the many cultures of the world in the same way. A cultural Buddhist can be a follower of Jesus. A cultural Moslem can be a follower of Jesus. It's just like a cultural Catholic can be a follower of Jesus without renouncing his cultural background or a cultural Baptist or a cultural Methodist. Anyone can be a follower of Jesus and still remain within his or her cultural background. Jesus demonstrated this with every encounter.

Christianity isn't the way, the truth, and the life.

The Church isn't the way, the truth, and the life.

Jesus is!

CHAPTER 8

Does Jesus Trump Everything?

At the Dalai Lama event where I spoke in San Francisco, Diana sat next to a man who has worked closely with His Holiness, especially in helping his people in and out of Tibet. He embraces the Buddhist way of life and has been highly successful in his business ventures over the years. She didn't tell him that her husband was one of the speakers on the platform (I think she needed an out, if I wasn't received well.).

As I noted before, I was the last to be introduced. When it was clear to her that I was being warmly received, especially by her new friend, she whispered, "That's my husband." As soon as I finished and the entire gathering was dismissed, he made his way up to me with such enthusiasm. He said, "I've never heard about Jesus in this way ever in my life! I love it! I think to sum up your remarks I would say, 'Jesus trumps everything!'"

I wholeheartedly agreed.

But does he? Does Jesus trump *everything?*

Let's take a look at four crucial areas and see for ourselves.

One—Jesus Came to Restore What Man Has Lost

Jesus restores mankind back to Eden. In the well-known Garden of Eden story, Adam and Eve enjoyed the presence of God. They were all set—good jobs, lush place to live, great retirement benefits, and a personal relationship with God.

They were to fulfill three purposes:
- Together they were to reflect the image of the Creator-God.

- They were to reproduce that image by filling the earth with children.

- They were to reign together against evil to cultivate and guard the garden as co-rulers with Him.

Both made a fatal mistake, not only in failing God, but in failing each other. They had only one prohibition that was set up by God. However one wants to characterize that prohibition and the subsequent encounter with the serpent that lured them into breaking the universal law set up by their Creator, *they blew it!*

They blew it by not trusting their Creator-God and disobeying what He said. What's interesting is that by disobeying Him they not only broke the law, but the law broke them. They were expelled from the Garden with three definitive consequences:
- They lost the Kingdom where they were co-rulers with their Creator.

- They lost the personal relationship with the Creator-God.

- They lost the abiding presence of God's Spirit.

Ever since those losses humankind has been desperately trying to recover. It seems that the hole in the soul of every man and woman can be attributed to those three losses—the Kingdom of God, a personal relationship with God, and God's abiding presence through His Spirit. They didn't lose heaven, but they did give up the Kingdom, their personal relationship with God, and His abiding presence with them on earth.

Since that epic rebellion against the Creator-God,

the very things people were supposed to rule over have enslaved them:

- *Plants* have been used to produce a variety of drugs and alcohol to be abused with the end result of being addicted and controlled by them.

- *Passions* in humankind have gotten rampantly out of control to the point of people living life lustily rather than passionately.

- *Possessions* have easily taken a prominent place in our lives and we live under the deception that people, places, and things can make us happy. All of these promise so much more than they can deliver.

Every religion, philosophy, and political ideology is an attempt to fill that hole in the soul, where there is a deep yearning for fulfillment and joy . . .

- To seek the Kingdom that was lost in the Garden.

- To seek to re-establish a personal relationship with the Creator.

- To seek to restore the abiding presence of God.

Most every religion is setting up a system and often an obstacle course to make your way through in order to get out of this painful place and get out of here—to Heaven, Nirvana, Eden, Shangri-la, Paradise, or the Promised Land. Every religious system is a well-meaning attempt with its desires and standards. Christians are trying to be the best Christians, Buddhists the best Buddhists, as are Hindus, Moslems, Jews, and Animists. Since God created all peoples and is holding them together, eternity has been placed in everyone's heart. This is why people worldwide search for God. At the core of this search is this deep ache from the hole in the soul. Everyone is seeking the Kingdom, seeking that personal relationship with the Creator-God, and seeking an abiding presence with God as in the beginning in the Garden of Eden.

But setting up ways to get out of here isn't the way of God; it's the way of man. Nor is it God's way to set up a system of do's and don'ts to avoid going to hell. It's interesting to note that there was no system set up in the Garden of Eden and no worship, but only a relationship with the Creator-God, walking together in the Garden. This is why, after establishing a massive system of sacrifices and feasts, God says through the prophets, "I want compassion rather than your sacrifices." God wants a relationship. There is a simple distinction made between religion and relationship. Religion is man's best attempt to avoid going to hell. Relationship says, "I've already been to hell and don't want to go back!"

Religion is man's idea.

Relationship is God's idea.

After being taught and teaching otherwise, I've come to the conclusion that God never intends to take those who respond to him out of here. Even with Jesus' teachings about his return and the end of the world, he has not given us a way to get out of here. That's not the direction! God is doing all he can to get down here—to dwell among us. So, this is what God has been up to ever since man lost *the Kingdom, the personal relationship, and the abiding presence of God.* Through the priests, the judges, the kings, and the prophets God wanted to dwell among those who would trust him and those people would be a blessing to all the nations of the world.

After the prophets, there was a period of 400 silent years. It was at this point that Jesus was sent to earth. His mission was to reveal the *Good News of the Kingdom* and by doing this to restore what mankind had lost. Jesus repeatedly announced the Kingdom, he established the personal relationship, and he introduced the abiding presence of

God for all to experience.

Jesus brought the Kingdom of God to earth, because he is the King. Wherever the King is, there is the Kingdom. He was the dwelling place of God on earth, fully indwelt with the Spirit of God. God had finally come down here to dwell among those who would trust Him.

Jesus did one more amazing thing. He re-introduced the Spirit of God as the abiding presence of God—to permanently indwell people again as in the Garden. With this introduction it is again possible to enjoy a personal relationship with the Creator-God—to walk with him in the Garden. So the Kingdom, the personal relationship with God, and his abiding presence are no longer things hoped for, but they have become a reality in Jesus. They're not enjoyed in a lush garden any longer. They are experienced right here, right now—an inner peace in the context of broken pieces.

He came to turn religious stress into rest. Jesus said, "Come to me, all you who are weary and burdened, and I will give you rest. Take my yoke upon you and learn from me, for I am gentle and humble in heart, and you will find rest for your souls. For my yoke is easy and my burden is light." You can have all that was ever lost in the Garden. Jesus can fill up the hole in your soul. Jesus can restore what mankind has lost. It's all about restoration and transformation. Restoration and transformation cannot be acquired on your own.

Two—Jesus Came to Give You What You Can't Get on Your Own

What is it that Jesus can give you that you can't get on your own? This may sound a bit strange, but Jesus came as a revolutionary. The revolution is all about restoration and transformation.

My entire professional life I have worked with people

at their deepest needs. I jokingly say, "I've counseled half of Orange County since 1975, and I feel like the other half is coming in this month." When you grapple with people's problems, it doesn't take long to see what they are.

For too long I believed I had the answers to their needs and struggles. I didn't! The bottom line is I could only suggest some tools for them to help themselves. But, at best, these wonderful tools enable a person to achieve a level of reformation by reforming themselves. Certainly this is helpful, but reformation can only work with symptoms. Transformation is what is needed at the core level— an inner change of heart.

Since I've been following Jesus I have found four experiences that have become amazingly real to me. On the negative side of the emotional ledger we humans are continually struggling with fear, anger, guilt, and shame.

Jesus offers a positive counter-experience to each of these toxic emotions.

- Peace that counteracts the fear!

- Love that counteracts the anger!

- Joy that counteracts the guilt!

- Grace that counteracts the shame!

And what is even more amazing is that we are hearing these same experiences shared among those who are fighting the toughest battles. They are fighting the experiences of betrayal, divorce, death of a loved one, fighting the ongoing treatment of cancer, international peace negotiations, and financial disasters. They are fighting in the military, families being torn apart. They are surviving the wearisome conflicts of others, along with a variety of addictions.

What is really needed is a genuine change of heart— to see your life, predicaments, and people differently. Several years ago, we set out to study only the five Gospels for three years—Matthew, Mark, Luke, John, and Acts. We did this in order to get to know this Jesus. This focus proved to be life changing! It was through this Jesus journey that we discovered what only Jesus could do for us that we cannot do for ourselves. I have no capability to change a person's heart. I can't give people peace. I can't give people joy. I can't give them love. I can't, but I've come to realize that Jesus can!

Again, I am not speaking of the religious Jesus. I am referring to the most prominent and powerful person ever! And, in the most pragmatic way, this Jesus seems to be able to affect these internal changes in people. Even though I have experienced this personally and have observed his effect in people who need what he has, I find myself caught up in the joy of actually seeing it happen.

There's something about Jesus without religious baggage—his words, his actions, his loving ways, his bent toward the disenfranchised and especially his name—that brings healing and wholeness to the heart and mind. Jesus is truly the most effective person you can embrace for yourself.

Here are the four life-transforming experiences we are finding in Jesus:

The Experience of Peace. Jesus was all about peace. Peace is not just absence of conflict or a cessation of the battles waging in us and around us. It's a sense of inner calm that all is going to be alright.

When Jesus first sent his disciples out, he sent them to go into villages and give the blessing of peace to those who were interested (Matthew 10). Frequently, Jesus said to troubled people, "Go in peace."

At the last gathering of Jesus' disciples before his death, Jesus said, "Peace I leave with you; my peace I give to you; not as the world gives do I give to you. Do not let your heart be troubled, nor let it be fearful" (John 14). And later in that gathering he said, "These things I have spoken to you, so that in me you may have peace" (John 16).

After his death and resurrection, Jesus appears to his disciples and set them up for a special mission. Jesus says, "Peace be with you! As the Father has sent me, I am sending you" (John 20). As soon as Jesus said this he empowered them to go into the world and bring peace to everyone they meet. Jesus brought peace to everyone he met. Now he is sending out all of his followers to do the same—to be peacemakers—agents of reconciliation wherever they go.

One of our closest friends with whom we have been doing life together for many years was struck with a rare form of cancer. Jeff is enduring a variety of chemo and radiation treatments and struggles with the depressing results of his fight. He had tried his best to find peace through many channels. He has only found genuine peace through personal interaction with Jesus. Now he is teaching all of us what it means to embrace this peace.

Through Jesus *peace* is available to anyone who wants it. This is the kind of peace that you just can't get on your own.

The Experience of Joy. Joy is different from happiness. Joy is deeper than that. Happiness depends upon the happenings that are going on right now. Joy is an inner quality of seeing things with a positive perspective. Joy is the ability to enjoy the scenery, when you are on a detour!

When Jesus was born, it was announced that he was to be the good news of great joy for all people (Luke 2). Then, at that special final gathering with his disciples Jesus says, "These things I have spoken to you so that my joy may be in you, and that your joy may be made full" (John 15). Jesus was teaching them about their relationship with him, that it is as vital as a branch connected to the vine. As a follower remains connected to Jesus, he will experience the same joy Jesus possessed. Think of it! You can have Jesus' joy in you in all its brimming fullness, spilling over into every area of your life and into the lives of others!

Jesus even challenged his followers by saying, "Until now you have asked for nothing in my name; ask and you will receive, so that your joy may be made full" (John 16). And as Jesus prays he says, "But now I come to You; and these things I speak in the world so that they may have my joy made full in themselves" (John 17).

Do you get the picture that Jesus is bent on his followers experiencing joy? Through Jesus, joy is available to anyone who wants it.

The Experience of Love. Although peace and joy are commonly identified with Jesus, love is the theme of who Jesus is and what he taught. Most Christian children know the song, "Jesus loves me, this I know." Jesus is the epitome of love. To act like Jesus is to do the loving thing.

Jesus taught that his followers ought to learn to love God. He said, "You shall love the Lord your God with all your heart, and with all your soul, and with all your mind, and with all your strength" (Matthew 22). This concept provides a centering effect in your life.

There's something very fundamental about loving someone greater than your self—something of an inner balance that keeps you and your life in proper perspective.

Along with loving God Jesus taught his followers to love your neighbor. He says, "You shall love your neighbor as yourself" (Matthew 22). Jesus' teaching on loving your neighbor requires you to love anyone in need. After sharing these two loves, Jesus says there is no commandment greater than these two.

Jesus goes further in his teachings on love by instructing his followers to love one another, whether they were in need of anything or not. He says to his disciples, "A new commandment I give to you, that you love one another, even as I have loved you, that you also love one another. By this all men will know that you are my disciples, if you have love for one another" (John 13). To Jesus this experience of love is not just to love God and to love your neighbor, but to love one another. Loving one another is to be the mark of one who is a follower of Jesus.

Next, Jesus extends this love theme to include your enemies. You want to know how to eliminate your enemies? Love them! Jesus says, "But I say to you who hear, love your enemies, do good to those who hate you. If you love those who love you, what credit is that to you? For even sinners love those who love them. But love your enemies, and do good, and lend, expecting nothing in return; and your reward will be great, and you will be sons of the Most High; for He Himself is kind to ungrateful and evil men" (Luke 6).

Jesus-style love ranges from loving God, loving your neighbor, loving one another, and even to the extreme of loving your enemies. What's most convicting to me is that this experience of love is not just an emotional state of being. It's a state of doing, whether you feel it or not.

As I said before . . . we don't need more love; we need more lovers!

Jesus views our commitment to follow him within a loving relationship. "Just as the Father has loved me, I have also loved you; abide in my love. If you keep my commandments, you will abide in my love; just as I have kept my Father's commandments and abide in His love. This is my commandment, that you love one another, just as I have loved you" (John 15). Keeping his commandments means to walk in his steps—to follow his example and teachings.

This love relationship is so tight that a follower of Jesus can actually own the love of God in himself. Jesus says, "I in them and You in me, that my followers may be perfected in unity, so that the world may know that You sent me, and loved them, even as You have loved me....so that the love with which you loved me may be in them and I in them" (John 17).

Wow! I read these teachings of Jesus and wonder what went wrong. Jesus wants all of his followers to live in unity—to be one—to love one another. Yet, for the most part, we are divided. And worse, we are proud of it

The Experience of Grace. Karma, which is another way of saying that we reap what we sow—is a reality. There are always consequences for our actions. But there is something that trumps karma—grace. Grace is something you don't deserve, something you didn't work for, something you weren't able to plan for or to orchestrate. Grace is given by Jesus, many times with no rhyme or reason to it.

Grace is one of the primary themes of Jesus as he touches the untouchable lepers and the unclean, as he opens the eyes of the blind, as he has compassion on the poor and the disenfranchised, as he receives those who are on the outside of the religious world, as he welcomes women and children—those normally pushed aside, and as he chooses the ordinary, uneducated to be the leaders of his movement. Just as grace trumps karma, so does Jesus, the deliverer of grace, trump everything!

Two of the dynamics within the experience of grace are forgiveness and freedom. It's hard to imagine two more powerful life principles than these. And these two dynamics are in tandem with one another.

Every time I bring up the subject of forgiveness, people immediately wake up and take notes. So many are locked up in the state of unforgiveness. Either they long to be forgiven for something they have done or not done or they are imprisoned by not being willing to forgive someone who has hurt them. Either way, people are stuck in unforgiveness.

Once you forgive another person, you set a prisoner free. That prisoner is *you.* Once you experience forgiveness, either by forgiving or being forgiven, you enter into a wonderful sense of freedom.

Several of the most popular radio therapists don't even have forgiveness in their repertoire. This is why they may do a lot of good, but when it comes to really setting people free, they can only put the equivalent of bandages on compound fractures.

Forgiveness and freedom are two of Jesus' most powerful principles in his repertoire. Paul, an early follower of Jesus, spoke in a synagogue in Asia Minor to God-fearing Jews and non-Jews as a guest speaker (Acts 13). He said, "I want you to know two things. Through Jesus is forgiveness and through Jesus is the kind of freedom the Law of Moses couldn't provide."

Through Jesus grace is available to anyone who wants it. This is the kind of grace that you just can't get on your own.

All kinds of religious systems and programs offer you lots of things, but Jesus can give you true and lasting peace, joy, love, and grace.

Three—Jesus Came to Personalize the God of Gods

Remember the C. S. Lewis story of God writing himself into the play of life through the character of Jesus? The third observation of how Jesus trumps everything is playing out this character.

Have you ever tried to follow God? Not easy, is it? God seems so out there, so unknowable, but we're not able to know God completely due to our human limitations. How is it possible to be God-like in our lifestyles?

Jesus came to personalize the God of the universe. Jesus came to introduce mankind to him. Jesus came to clarify this God. Jesus invites any who will to follow and get to know this God. It's like Jesus is the point person—the way to know this God.

Some have told me that the phrase "Jesus plus nothing" just isn't accurate. Their concerns are that using "Jesus plus nothing" pushes God and his Spirit aside to a lesser role. This just isn't so.

I want to walk you through why I see "Jesus plus nothing" as the most accurate way of positioning Jesus. Those of you who know the Bible will see clearly what I'm saying. For those of you who don't know the Bible that well, I think you will see how pre-eminent Jesus is presented by the New Testament writers.

Paul wrote a letter to the followers of Jesus in Colossae and made a case for Jesus embodying all of the fullness of God. He says, "He was supreme in the beginning and—leading the resurrection parade—he is supreme in the end. From beginning to end he's there, towering far above everything, everyone. So spacious is he, so roomy, that everything of God finds its proper place in him without crowding. Not only that, but all the broken and dislocated pieces of the universe—people and things, animals and atoms—get properly fixed and fit together in vibrant harmonies" (Colossians 1, *The Message*).

He continues, "Everything of God gets expressed in him, so you can see and hear him clearly. You don't need a telescope, a microscope, or a horoscope to realize the fullness of Jesus, and the emptiness of the universe without him. When you come to him, that fullness comes together for you, too. His power extends over everything" (Colossians 2, *The Message*).

All of the fullness of God dwells in Jesus in bodily form. It's all in Jesus—Jesus plus nothing else!

In the opening chapter of the Gospel of John, John writes about Jesus, "In the beginning was the Word, and the Word was with God, and the Word was God. He was with God in the beginning. Through him all things were made; without him nothing was made that has been made. In him was life, and that life was the light of all people. The light shines in the darkness, and the darkness has not overcome it. The true light that gives light to everyone was coming into the world. He was in the world and though the world was made through him, the world did not recognize him. He came to that which was his own, but his own did not receive him. Yet to all who did receive him, to those who believed in his name, he gave the right to become children of God—children born not of natural descent, nor of human decision or a husband's will, but born of God. The Word became flesh and made his dwelling among us. We have seen his glory, the glory of the one and only Son, who came from the Father, full of grace and truth . . . . Out of his fullness we have all received grace in place of grace already given. For the law was given through Moses. Grace and truth came through Jesus Christ. No one has ever seen God, but the one and only Son, who is himself God and is in closest relationship with the Father, has made him known" (John 1).

Not even the written Word is equal to Jesus. Jesus states this clearly to the religious leaders when he said, "You study the Scriptures diligently, because you think that in them you possess eternal life. These are the very Scriptures that testify about me, yet you refuse to come to me to have life" (John 5).

There is a powerfully insightful teaching of Jesus we'll discuss later, but it's important to list it here to get the point of Jesus plus nothing. Jesus says, "I am the true vine, and my Father is the gardener. He lifts up every branch in me that bears no fruit, while every branch that does bear fruit he prunes so that it will be even more fruitful. Remain in me, as I also remain in you. No branch can bear fruit by itself; it must remain in the vine. Neither can you bear fruit unless you remain in me. I am the vine; you are the branches. If you remain in me and I in you, you will bear much fruit; apart from me you can do nothing" (John 15). This all happens in the name of Jesus with nothing added. Not Miracle Grow on the leaves. Not mulch on the roots. Just Jesus. Note that it's not without the Spirit you can do nothing, but without Jesus you can do nothing. You just can't short-change this. It is clearly Jesus plus nothing!

Check out what Jesus says of the Spirit and the Father here: "I have much more to say to you, more than you can now bear. But when he, the Spirit of truth, comes, he will guide you into all the truth. He will not speak on his own; he will speak only what he hears, and he will tell you what is yet to come. He will glorify me, because it is from me that he will receive what he will make known to you. All that belongs to the Father is mine. That is why I said the Spirit will receive from me what he will make known to you" (John 16).

Do you see the pre-eminence of Jesus acted out in the play?

He is the marquee character.

And the spotlight is always on him.

Four—Jesus Dissolves Alienation at Every Level

About eight years ago when Jesus apprehended my wife's and my heart in a fresh way, we were struggling with how to say what we do. I had resigned as a pastor and drastically curtailed the speaking engagements in order to authentically walk with Jesus and to walk with others on this spiritual journey. So at this juncture I struggled with what I would say when someone asks, "What do you do?"

I had just left a long luncheon in Arlington, Virginia, where a few men going in the same direction shared with me the kinds of things they shared when asked that question. The one angle I latched on to was, "I work with the problem of alienation." I don't know why, but that seemed an attractive handle to me.

When I checked out of the hotel, I asked the front desk to call me a taxi. The woman at the desk suggested that I take a town car instead for the same price. We were also in the middle of a serious snowstorm, so the town car made sense. When the car arrived, the driver was a large man from Cameroon, Africa. His name was Joseph Nkodo.

On our way, he asked, "What do you do?"

"I work with the problem of alienation."

I thought this will bring any conversation to a halt.

"Oh, alienation," he said, "like between countries and families and villages. How do you work with alienation? What can you do?"

"Well, we don't approach it politically, educationally, or religiously. We have found that the best answers to the problem of alienation are the teachings and principles of Jesus." I found it difficult to get the name of Jesus out of my mouth. It was the weirdest, yet most wonderful, thing. I'd never just presented Jesus to a person.

Joseph didn't skip a beat. "Oh, Jesus. You know, in my country you grow up either Muslim or Catholic. However, it really doesn't matter, because everyone worships their ancestors anyway. But I've always thought Jesus was so different from everything else." Joseph from Cameroon taught me how to speak about Jesus. Joseph and his family have become good friends of ours and they know what it means to follow Jesus.

Since that initiation experience, I've spoken with others on alienation quite often. More often, though I find myself just sharing illustrations of Jesus, dissolving the problem of alienation here and now. Here are several that come to mind:

Jesus trumps competition between denominations and religions. There is a variety of church cultures that are part of the Christian community. Jesus prayed for all followers to be one in his love, yet Christians tend toward being divisive, competitive, and condemning. This causes alienation.

How sad that Christians are so fragmented. My own narrow Baptist roots were so fragmented that we didn't even accept other Baptists. When it came to Catholics, we felt we had nothing to discuss with them. Early on when embracing Jesus plus nothing, the Catholic Diocese of Orange County invited me to conduct a three-hour training session on how to reach disenchanted Catholics. What an opportunity this was to share the simplicity of following Jesus! We do have so much in common, if we keep the main thing the main thing. Which is Jesus. Simply Jesus.

This oneness for which Jesus prayed goes beyond the Western Christian culture. We are brothers and sisters with all those who are followers of Jesus, whether Mormon, Jehovah's Witness, Buddhist, Adventist, Hindu, Baptist, Church of Christ, Jew, Muslim, or whatever. I wish I had a dollar for every time someone asked me to help them understand some other religious system. What they are really asking is, "What are the differences, and how can I argue my beliefs over theirs?" Instead, we must find a common ground of unity in Jesus. There is no barrier between us no matter who it is, if we are both discussing Jesus. The Jesus movement includes all who God is calling to Himself from every culture.

Jesus trumps the animosity between political parties. One of our privileges in life is to be able to participate in the President's National Prayer Breakfast each year. Representatives from around 150-160 nations come and gather in the name of Jesus to pray. Political alienation and fighting is all we hear about in the daily news, yet we rarely hear of the many from the political right and left who have discovered and experienced unity in Jesus. So many of these Congressmen and Senators have carved out a very close family friendship through coming together and learning to follow Jesus as the one who matters most in their lives. Their love for one another is a beautiful thing to watch!

Jesus trumps prejudicial conflict. A few years ago we had a local judge who was brought up on charges of having child porn on his computer. It was the major scandal for the feeding frenzy of the media for quite some time. Los

Angeles radio stations sponsored demonstrations from his front yard. It was ugly! When the judge and I met together, I suggested that he can't go through this alienation from others alone. I invited him to come to a weekly study at our training center. We had about 100 women and 50 men who were going through this particular study. Since he was under house arrest and wore a security anklet, he had to get permission to attend.

The night he showed up, I purposefully placed him at a table where my best friend was the table leader and sat him in between a former Irvine Police Detective, whose primary area was pornography, and an opinionated former Marine, who preferred to shoot first, then ask questions. No one, except my best buddy, knew this was the judge in the news. As these men around the table finally realized who was at their table, the love and unifying dynamic of Jesus overwhelmed them. They found the power through Jesus to embrace the judge as a brother.

By the way, in that study we had two men who were wearing security anklets. Jesus trumped the prejudice that might have been a natural response and exchanged it with his love.

Jesus trumps marital differences. Dear friends of mine have a wonderful story about how Jesus can change a marriage. The husband is a Muslim and his wife is a Catholic. They fell so deeply in love that they didn't count the cost of any religious consequences in the marriage later, especially when children came along.

Their marriage was filled with sniping and bickering causing serious alienation over these religious and cultural differences. To put it mildly, they were not enjoying their marriage; at best, they were enduring it. They met a friend of mine and shared with him the marital struggles they were experiencing and he gave them a solution that has worked marvelously over the years. He said, "Why don't you both start following Jesus and unify yourselves around your relationship with him?" Well, they did, and the transformation has been dramatic!

That's the power of Jesus plus nothing!

Jesus trumps natural enemies. Recently we met two women who were bitter enemies by no fault of their own. You see, one woman's son murdered the son of the other. Both women loved God, yet here they were, both with broken hearts without any way out of this cycle of pain. They had never spoken before. Then, one day in the hallways of the courthouse, they saw one another, stopped, and sobbed in one another's arms. Jesus has now knit their hearts together as the dearest of friends, and they are ministering to others who find themselves in the same situation.

Jesus trumps the alienation you are experiencing personally.

- Are you alienated from yourself?
- Are you alienated from God?
- Are you alienated from your spouse?
- Are you alienated from your children?
- Are you alienated from your parents?
- Are you alienated from your friends?
- Are you alienated from your neighbors?
- Are you alienated from your colleagues?
- Are you alienated from your enemies?

As is with most of our personal problems the bottom-line solution comes down to one thing—*surrender.* But surrender to what or to whom? Surrender doesn't work in vague terms. Some say, for example, that you must surrender to the "universe," but surrender works best when you can identify where to submit your alienation. And we have found it best to surrender your will and your life over to Jesus.

We know a man who was recently struggling with life and death issues in a psych ward at a local hospital. He asked to be restrained so that he couldn't hurt himself or others. He knew he had to give up the anxiety, but didn't know where to go. His wife suggested that he surrender to Jesus. He did and found the first extended period of rest he had in several days. Jesus can bridge every form of alienation you are experiencing.

He alone brings unity, peace, reconciliation.

As my Buddhist friend said, "Jesus trumps everything!"

Part III

the presence of the kingdom

CHAPTER 9

Did Jesus Launch a Church or a Movement?

Jesus mentions the term "church" on only two occasions, which comes as a surprise to many. He spends most of his time teaching about the Kingdom. But despite his emphasis, we spend most of our time talking about the Church and almost no time talking about the Kingdom.

It's not that the Kingdom has been rejected, but reduced by what is typically taught. There are, at least, five ways that we tend to reduce the Kingdom.

The first way the Kingdom is reduced is when we call it mystical. If it's mystical, then it is very difficult to explain and understand definitively. It's sort of other-worldly.

Second, many describe the Kingdom as heavenly. This is a lot like the first. If the Kingdom is heavenly, then it has little, if any, application on earth.

The third way the Kingdom is reduced is when we see it as apocalyptic. This means it isn't for today, but is relegated to a time in the future when Jesus will set up his Kingdom on earth.

The fourth way the Kingdom is reduced is when it is equated to the Church. Many see the Kingdom as the local church and therefore it's limited to whether it's a good and healthy church or not.

Finally, the Kingdom is reduced when we define it as acts of social concern. To many, feeding the poor and doing charitable deeds among the needy is where the Kingdom is.

There is a little bit of each of these dimensions that is true, but the Kingdom cannot be defined by any one of them alone. The way Jesus teaches, the Kingdom is greater than anything that has ever existed on earth. Jesus makes it clear that the Kingdom is near—within reach—here and among us right now, and there seems to be a time in the future when the Kingdom will be more fully experienced on earth.

Since Jesus is the King, his teachings and very presence brought the Kingdom to earth for us. Once you embrace the fact that the presence of the Kingdom is *right here, right now*, you can begin enjoying yourself as you live in the Kingdom *right here, right now*. You embrace the Kingdom lifestyle by living out the teachings and principles of the King and his Kingdom. Jesus calls it following him or doing the will of the Father or hearing his words and practicing them.

In other words, you can live in the Kingdom today, right now. When you embrace the Kingdom lifestyle, you may find yourself going against the grain and the natural flow of the world. Don't forget that the world system Jesus spoke so often about included the religious leadership of the day. You will find yourself caught up in the flow of the movement of the Kingdom of God or better yet, you will be caught up in the 21st century Jesus movement. It's a revolutionary movement, and Jesus is the one who leads it. So, see where Jesus is at work and get there as soon as possible. Walk with him. Watch him. Work with him. No matter your circumstances, you can practice the presence of the Kingdom and enjoy the presence of the King—Jesus—*right here* on planet earth, *right now*.

Matthew records Jesus' first message: From that time on Jesus began to preach, "Repent, for the kingdom of heaven has come near" (Matthew 4).

When Jesus sent the twelve disciples out for their first mission, he said, "As you go, proclaim this message: 'The kingdom of heaven has come near,'" (Matthew 10). It was so close that it was within their reach.

Jesus carried this same theme of the Kingdom beyond his disciples. According to Luke 17:20-21, Jesus was addressing his remarks to the Pharisees: Once, having been asked by the Pharisees when the Kingdom of God would come, Jesus replied, "The coming of the Kingdom of God is not something that can be observed, nor will people say, 'Here it is,' or 'There it is,' because the Kingdom of God is in your midst." Another way of saying this is, "The Kingdom of God is in you or among you all." I think what Jesus is saying is that he has brought the Kingdom—the presence of God to earth. You see, where the King is, there is the Kingdom.

So, Jesus isn't about the Church and Jesus isn't about Christianity; Jesus is all about the Kingdom being among us right here today! The presence of the Kingdom is the second essential in breaking down the walls that keep people from Jesus.

From time to time we read through the book of Acts, reading each chapter according to the day of the month. In doing so, we begin to feel like we are getting caught up in the action of Jesus right here right now. One of the things that hit me when reading through Acts was that I noticed a definite theme throughout. Jesus (Acts 1), Philip (Acts 8), and Paul (Acts 28) all had the same teaching—Jesus and the Kingdom. Check it out!

Acts 1—Jesus. After Jesus' suffering, he presented himself to them and gave many convincing proofs that he was alive. He appeared to them over a period of forty days and spoke about the Kingdom of God. On one occasion, while he was eating with them, he gave them this command: "Do not leave Jerusalem, but wait for the gift my Father promised, which you have heard me speak about. For John baptized with water, but in a few days you will be baptized with the Holy Spirit. But you will receive power when the Holy Spirit comes on you; and you will be my witnesses in Jerusalem, and in all Judea and Samaria, and to the ends of the earth."

This is an interesting time with Jesus. Jesus spends 40 days with his disciples to do two things. He was there to prove to the disciples that he really was raised from the dead and spending that much time with them leaves no doubt in their minds. The second thing Jesus wanted to do was to teach them about the Kingdom of God. He spent most of his time with them for years teaching them about the Kingdom, but during that time they still thought the Kingdom was more of a political nature where the Roman domination would be obliterated. Jesus spent this time with them to make certain they really got it. It's all about Jesus and the Kingdom.

Acts 8—Philip. But when they believed Philip as he proclaimed the Good News of the Kingdom of God and the name of Jesus the Christ, they were baptized, both men and women.

Philip was one of the selected ministers who was to be working in the trenches. His message to the Samaritans was also two-fold. He was proclaiming the Good News of the Kingdom of God and the name of Jesus. There it is again—Jesus and the Kingdom.

Acts 28—Paul. They arranged to meet Paul on a certain day, and came in even larger numbers to the place where he was staying. He witnessed to them from morning till evening, explaining about the Kingdom of God, and from the Law of Moses and from the Prophets he tried to persuade them about Jesus. Some were convinced by what he said, but others would not believe.

For two whole years Paul stayed there in his own rented house and welcomed all who came to see him. He proclaimed the kingdom of God and taught about the Lord Jesus Christ—with all boldness and without hindrance!

At the end of Paul's life he was under house arrest in Rome. He lived in a rented house. While living there, all kinds of people came to visit him and he was able to continue his teaching while imprisoned in this way. Luke mentions it twice here that Paul also had a two-fold message—Jesus and the Kingdom.

So, are we missing out on something in our teaching today? I think we're missing Jesus and the Kingdom. Which raises a question. What exactly is the Kingdom?

What Is the Kingdom?

A kingdom is where someone rules—where you are the king of your dome or domain. Another way of seeing a kingdom is "what you have say over"—all your stuff. Each of us has a kingdom and you are king over your kingdom. However, when you encounter Jesus, the King of kings, you will want to step down as king and make Jesus your King. So the Kingdom of God is all that God has say over.

I like this simple definition of the Kingdom: wherever the king is, there is the Kingdom. You see, the presence of the Kingdom is the presence of Jesus. If you are going to walk with Jesus—the pre-eminent one, then it is essential that you walk in his presence or walk in the presence of the Kingdom where Jesus rules. Walking in the presence of the Kingdom is embracing the principles and teachings of Jesus as a lifestyle.

The Kingdom is not something you build; you must practice, live it, and *be* it. It's an alternative reality in this world. In fact, the Kingdom is built into nature—the very structure of our being. It's in our DNA. The Kingdom principles are the principles of life itself. Following these principles is how life works best. In other words, the Kingdom principles of Jesus are not foreign or some new lifestyle to be lived in this world. These principles are the way God created everyone to operate from the beginning. It's like the principle of gravity. On this planet gravity is in force, no matter how you feel about it or how much you understand. According to the principle of gravity, if you jump off a two-story building, you will go down fast, hit with a thud and you won't like it. No matter what you do, the gravity remains in place. If we were to vote down the principle of gravity, who would be crazy enough to try it out by jumping off the two-story building? Whoever it is will find that he will go down fast, hit with a thud, and he won't like it. You may not understand it, but you must learn to go along with it, or you may get hurt. You may try to break the law of gravity, but it will break you in the process. This is precisely how the principles of the Kingdom of God work.

I don't understand the principle of gravity, but I respect it. You may not understand electricity, but you use it and respect it.

These principles of life are natural laws of life—a fact of life. Once you understand that, you will understand that highly explosive concept of sin in a whole new way. Sin is defined as missing the mark. It is like an arrow falling short of its target. It is not what God created us to do; He wants us to be *on* target. If sin was part of our nature, then we would feel inwardly fulfilled when we sin without any guilt or regret. But we don't. Sin is an attempt to live against the laws of your being—the principles of the Kingdom—and get away with it.

Sin is missing the mark or falling short. What is the mark we're missing, the standard we're falling short of? The mark we're missing, the standard we're falling short of, is Jesus. He is the standard. He is the mark. The fullest embodiment of the Kingdom principles is in King Jesus, himself. He continues to make known his solution to missing the mark and falling short. It is not to believe something new, but to change the direction of your life to enjoy life to its fullest.

This is really the Good News! This is what Jesus calls the gospel or Good News of the Kingdom. This is why the subject of Jesus' first message was, "repent, for the Kingdom of heaven has come near." Note what Jesus began to proclaim to the people: "Repent or change your mind about what you're doing—wake up—for the Kingdom of heaven has come near." He begins his teaching with the Kingdom and ends it there with the disciples.

Jesus went all over, teaching in the local synagogues, proclaiming the "good news" of the Kingdom. His primary activity to demonstrate this "good news" of the Kingdom was to meet the various needs of the people—healing every disease and sickness among them. The message of Jesus was the Good News of the Kingdom. Those who were attracted to this message were attracted to the Kingdom. They weren't looking for a new Rabbi to come along and plant new synagogues in their villages. And, these new disciples of Jesus were following Jesus as the King and were thrilled with the message of the Kingdom.

The people of Jesus' time were hoping for the Kingdom, but were viewing its coming with more of a political impact to get them out from under the Romans. They were missing out on what the true Good News of the Kingdom was, until Jesus came to demonstrate it. Today, I believe we are also missing the point of the Kingdom and therefore missing the joy of practicing the presence of the Kingdom now. So, then as now, the Kingdom concept is not rejected, but reduced from what God intends.

What Do You Have to Do to Enter the Kingdom?

One of the most fascinating things about Jesus' teachings is his perspective on who gets into the Kingdom and who doesn't. We all have our own ideas of who will enter the Kingdom and who will not. I want to show you what Jesus said and what I've come to understand these words to mean.

Internal Righteousness—A Matter of The Heart. Jesus

141

says, "For I tell you that unless your righteousness surpasses that of the Pharisees and the teachers of the law, you will certainly not enter the kingdom of heaven" (Matthew 5).

At the time Jesus walked on earth, the Pharisees and the teachers of the law made an external show of religiosity, but in their hearts were the opposite of what they portrayed. This external show was their ticket to enter the Kingdom of God. Jesus warned about allowing yourself to be caught up in the religiosity of following a list or system of do's and don'ts, thinking you are impressing God while you are impressing others. Jesus makes it clear that he is not impressed with this kind of thing, so don't you be! Jesus makes entering the Kingdom all about the heart.

Do The Will of My Father. Jesus says, "Not everyone who says to me, 'Lord, Lord,' will enter the kingdom of heaven, but only he who does the will of my Father who is in heaven" (Matthew 7).

If you keep reading, the context is fascinating! Jesus states, "Many will say to me on that day, 'Lord, Lord, did we not prophesy in your name and in your name drive out demons and in your name perform many miracles?' Then I will tell them plainly, 'I never knew you. Away from me, you evildoers!" (Matthew 7).

In the next paragraph Jesus seems to illustrate what he means by "doing the will of my Father," when he says: "Therefore everyone who hears these words of mine and puts them into practice is like a wise man who built his house on the rock. The rain came down, the streams rose, and the winds blew and beat against that house; yet it did not fall, because it had its foundation on the rock. But everyone who hears these words of mine and does not put them into practice is like a foolish man who built his house on sand. The rain came down, the streams rose, and the winds blew and beat against that house, and it fell with a great crash."

"Only those who do the will of my Father" seems to

mean "hearing the words of Jesus and putting them into practice." Only those who do this will enter the Kingdom.

Be Like a Child. Jesus says, "I tell you the truth, unless you change and become like little children, you will never enter the kingdom of heaven" (Matthew 18).

Then, again Jesus says: "I tell you the truth, anyone who will not receive the kingdom of God like a little child will never enter it." Luke repeats these exact words of Jesus. Jesus obviously taught this same theme frequently (Mark 10; Luke 18).

Then, in the Gospel of John, in an interaction with Nicodemus, Jesus uses a little different metaphor to say the same thing. Jesus says, "Very truly I tell you, no one can see the kingdom of God without being born again . . . . No one can enter the kingdom of God unless he is born of water and the Spirit." He goes on to say: "That which is born of the flesh is flesh and that which is born of the spirit is spirit" (John 3).

Being "born again" is essentially illustrating his theme of being like a child. As a very religious man, Nicodemus had too many add-ons, therefore he needed to be born all over again in order to be like a little child, so that he could enter the Kingdom.

As a spiritual child, you want to learn all you can about this new life with Jesus. As a spiritual child, you need to learn the ABCs of walking with Jesus. As a spiritual child, it's most helpful to watch Jesus carefully and mimic what you hear and see. As a spiritual child, you want to learn to simply trust Jesus with your life.

Difficult for Rich Man to Enter. Let's back up and see the story unfold.

A man came up to Jesus and asked, "Teacher, what good thing must I do to get eternal life?"

"Why do you ask me about what is good?" Jesus replied. "There is only One who is good. If you want to enter life, keep the commandments."

"Which ones?" he inquired.

Jesus replied, "you shall not murder, you shall not commit adultery, you shall not steal, you shall not give false testimony, honor your father and mother,' and 'love your neighbor as yourself.'" (Jesus equates eternal life with entering life or really living, then later in this passage he speaks of entering the Kingdom of God.)

The young man shockingly states: "All these I have kept," the young man said. "What do I still lack?"

Jesus answered, "If you want to be perfect, go, sell your possessions and give to the poor, and you will have treasure in heaven. Then come, follow me" (Luke 18). By "perfect" Jesus means to be complete and whole in your search for life.

Then, Jesus makes the following observation recorded in Matthew, Mark, and Luke: Jesus says to his disciples, "I tell you the truth, it is hard for a rich man to enter the kingdom of heaven. Again I tell you, it is easier for a camel to go through the eye of a needle than for a rich man to enter the kingdom of God" (Matthew 19).

Then, again, Jesus looked around and said to his disciples, "Children, how hard it is to enter the kingdom of God! It is easier for a camel (or rope in some translations) to go through the eye of a needle than for a rich man to enter the kingdom of God" (Mark 10; Luke 18). The disciples were amazed at his words. But Jesus said again, "How hard it is for the rich to enter the kingdom of God!"

Whether the image here truly is a camel or a rope going through the eye of a needle, the essence of what Jesus is saying is still the same. It is impossible for a rich man to enter into the Kingdom through his performance and wealth! The difficulty for the rich person is that he tends to trust in his riches for security and tends to think that people, places and things can make him happy or whole and complete.

Jesus speaks to this impossibility in this conversation with the disciples: "When the disciples overheard this, they were greatly astonished and asked, 'Who then can be saved?' Jesus looked at them and said, 'With human beings being saved or entering the Kingdom is impossible, but with God all things are possible" (Matthew 19).

Do you want to enter the Kingdom of God? Who do you depend on—your bank account, your stuff, or God? If you are rich and have a lot of stuff, then hold on to that stuff "loosely," so that you are not trusting in your riches, but in God for a complete and full eternal life and entrance into the Kingdom.

Sinners Will Enter First. The final reference Jesus made concerning what it takes to enter or not enter the Kingdom of God has a couple of dimensions. Both of these dimensions are direct warnings toward the religious. The first dimension: Jesus said to them, "I tell you the truth, the tax collectors and the prostitutes are entering the kingdom of God ahead of you. For John came to you to show you the way of righteousness, and you did not believe him, but the tax collectors and the prostitutes did. And even after you saw this, you did not repent and believe him" (Matthew 21).

Beware of being so religious and self-righteous. Jesus became most disturbed and angry with those who didn't see their need for God—those who thought they were right and righteous because of their beliefs and practices. Those who see their need most are the ones who are actually entering the Kingdom right now ahead of the religious and the righteous. He is not just saying that the most despised tax collectors and prostitutes will enter the Kingdom someday, but that they are entering right now!

The second dimension: "Woe to you, teachers of the law and Pharisees, you hypocrites! You shut the kingdom of heaven in men's faces. You yourselves do not enter, nor will you let those enter who are trying to" (Matthew 23).

Note the specifics of what Jesus is saying here in Matthew 23. He is clearly saying that these religious leaders in positions of authority are not entering the Kingdom. He has made several observations at other times about the reasons why they will not enter the Kingdom, primarily it is their religious pride—that they know it all and know they are right.

Jesus points out that these religious leaders who are not entering the Kingdom are also stopping others from entering by shutting the door of the Kingdom of heaven in their faces. How is this done? I think it's done by continually setting up certain restrictions (hurdles or add-ons) and limitations on who can get in and who will not. I did this as a teenager. I had been taught that no one could come into a relationship with God, unless you go down front at the end of the church service. Either you go down front at the altar call or "invitation" or you won't get into heaven. In many discussions with my good friends I made this clear to them and basically kept them from entering the Kingdom. The man-made "rule" or "requirement" I had embraced served to be a major barrier to my friends being attracted to Jesus.

Recently a Buddhist friend of mine, seeking to know Jesus and his teachings, decided to attend a Bible study in her community. She went out and bought a Bible to read and take with her to the study. When she showed up, she was initially welcomed and then was told that she had the "wrong" Bible. At the Christian bookstore someone had suggested to her that she might enjoy starting out with *The Message*. Now, this group of Christians essentially shut the door of the Kingdom in this young lady's face. I don't think Jesus is well represented by shutting doors. He certainly didn't do it with the Samaritan woman at the well, and her Bible had only the first five books of the Jewish Bible. If anyone had the "wrong" Bible, you would think it would have been her, and yet Jesus never said a word about it.

To sum up, Jesus is saying those who don't have it together will enter the Kingdom first. Those who think they have it together through what they know and believe and what they do may not enter the Kingdom at all. And these religious "know-it-alls" tend to turn people off, which essentially shut others out of the Kingdom, too.

A couple of thoughts here: Don't deceive yourself into thinking that your religious system or your behavior will get you into the Kingdom. Don't divert others away from Jesus because of your dogmatic religious system.

So, What Does Jesus Want Us to Do with the Organized Church?

Jesus didn't come to launch the organized Church as we know it. He came to launch a movement—the Jesus movement, which is the Kingdom of God. The Jesus movement is the natural result of people who are following Jesus. They are moving with Jesus and with one another. The Kingdom is the rule of God on planet Earth both personally and in community. The church is a simple gathering together. The term "church" is not a special or holy word as many believe and teach. It literally means "called-out ones" and was used to describe city council meetings or any kind of assembly where people are called out to meet for a purpose. It simply is a gathering of followers of Jesus.

The simple gathering of followers of Jesus on any day and at any location is a church. These gatherings revolve around four ingredients—fellowship, food, prayer, and the apostles' teachings (Acts 2).

So, since the Kingdom is the rule and presence of God on planet earth, think of it as wherever the King is, there is the Kingdom. The King and the Kingdom are inseparable. Therefore a good way to view the Kingdom is *Jesus-likeness universalized.*

The Kingdom is universal. The church is local. It consists of a gathering of followers of Jesus who are seeking, sharing in, and spreading the message of Jesus and his Kingdom. The church is not everywhere, but localized and limited to those who choose to gather together. The Kingdom is everywhere and unlimited in its impact on society. The Kingdom is not waiting for a local gathering to be established in order to have its effect. The Kingdom is already there in every country and in every culture.

The Church tends to be an organization. The Kingdom tends to be a movement.

Jesus speaks of the Good News of the Kingdom, but he never speaks of the Good News of the organized Church.

The Kingdom is invisible. The organized Church is visible.

You must *go* to the Church. The Kingdom *goes with you* wherever you go.

The Church gathers and scatters. The Kingdom is always present with you.

You enter the Church by membership. You enter the Kingdom by following Jesus.

Jesus never commanded anyone to seek the Church. Jesus commanded everyone who follows him to seek the Kingdom.

The Church may or may not grow. The Kingdom is continually growing. Therefore the Church can be shut down, but the Kingdom cannot be.

The Church may have God present. The Kingdom is God's presence in those who follow Jesus.

Reading through the five gospels (Matthew, Mark, Luke, John, and Acts), it is clear what Jesus and the disciples did with the "organized Church." View the synagogue as the organized Church. There are three observations that seem most relevant to me. You don't find Jesus or the disciples bashing the synagogue (Church). You don't find Jesus or the disciples starting new synagogues (churches), because of inadequate teaching or worship. You find Jesus and the disciples going to the synagogues (churches) and then orbiting around them.

Several years ago I read a book, *Orbiting the Giant*

Hairball: A Corporate Fool's Guide to Surviving with Grace by Gordon MacKenzie. MacKenzie worked at Hallmark Greeting Cards for 30 years in the creative department. He found that he was unable to be very creative if he had to spend his time in corporate meetings. So he learned to orbit around the corporate bureaucracy and not be entangled in it, freeing him to create. He also makes it clear that the hairball was absolutely necessary. Without it there was nothing to power the orbit and the hairball paid the bills.

This is exactly what the early fellowships of Jesus did. They participated in the synagogue, yet they were in orbit around their synagogue, their communities and around the marketplace. They went to synagogue (church) every Sabbath, yet they were there for a higher purpose—a Kingdom purpose. They were there to introduce more and more people to the pre-eminence of Jesus. When interest was expressed, they invited them to eat together and practiced the presence of the Kingdom.

Most churches today realize how important it is to move their members into a smaller gathering, so they put a lot of energy into small groups. Some of these small groups practice the pre-eminence of Jesus and the presence of the Kingdom and some don't. If the groups gather in the name of Jesus and become more like family, Jesus shows up and great things happen. Small groups that are only study groups or small lecture groups tend to learn about Jesus and not get to know Jesus and his Kingdom community sitting around the room.

The Jesus movement is global. God is calling people from every culture of the world to personal transformation. I believe God is doing this through the irresistible Jesus and the irreversible Kingdom.

The Presence of the Kingdom

The pre-eminence of Jesus, the King, and the presence of the Kingdom are inseparable.

Jesus' character is the core of the Kingdom presence. The Kingdom is the only moral authority with any kind of power to change society. The organized Church is not capable of it. The Church changes from time to time. Sometimes it's effective and sometimes it's not. Leaders are morally good and leaders are morally flawed. So, at any given time, the Church will not be able to deliver an ongoing moral authority to the community. The Kingdom is constant. Its power and effectiveness depend upon its leader—Jesus. Therefore living in the Kingdom and inviting others to share in it is the only solution to transforming a broken culture.

Jesus' teachings lead to fulfillment and meaning in the Kingdom. Jesus is the ultimate standard and the Kingdom is the lifestyle of living this out in society. The lifestyle of Kingdom-living is where ultimate fulfillment and meaning reside. They are the laws of the universe. You cannot break the laws of the Kingdom, but they can break you. For instance, one of the laws of the Kingdom is to forgive those who have hurt you. If you refuse to live out this Kingdom principle, you will pay dearly for it. You will be bound by your lack of forgiveness. You will be eaten up with this unforgiving heart. By breaking the principle, you are broken. When living within the Kingdom, you are safe and free and most fulfilled.

The presence of God is within the presence of the Kingdom. Where better to discover a personal relationship with the God of gods than where He lives in His Kingdom. Most people only go to church at baptisms, marriages, and funerals—only to be hatched, matched, and dispatched. As followers of Jesus, practice the presence of the Kingdom. The Church of Jesus, where his followers gather, has the opportunity to touch the people in our world, rather than always inviting them to come to the organized Church, where they may or may not be spiritually touched at all. With this kind of practice of the Kingdom lifestyle, there are massive opportunities to plant the seeds of Jesus everywhere—his peace, his joy, his love, and his grace.

This is the original intent of the movement Jesus came to launch. It's simple! It's Jesus and his Kingdom!

Follow the King . . . and you'll discover the Kingdom.

Embrace the Kingdom lifestyle . . . and you'll find yourself in the arms of the King!

CHAPTER 10

What Are the Secrets Jesus Revealed About the Kingdom?

The more closely the disciples followed their master, Jesus, the more he revealed to them his intention and strategy. There were two shocking disclosures Jesus shared with his early followers. Both of them were not anticipated; they were counterintuitive. Both of them were about the Jesus movement—the presence and purpose of the Kingdom lifestyle Jesus came to offer—the new and better way of living life before God and mankind—and his personal strategy for this Kingdom.

The first counterintuitive proposition was that the Kingdom Jesus promoted had more to do with the power of personal transformation and service rather than the power of political overthrow and dominance. Having lived under the dominance of the Romans for so long, the early followers of Jesus saw Jesus as their political liberator, who would somehow lead a powerful movement that would free them from Rome's grip.

Instead, Jesus spent most of his time teaching and acting out a different strategy—a strategy of setting things right through physical and spiritual healing. Instead of instigating an uprising or war against enemies, he had an entirely different approach. Jesus had the audacity to promote eliminating his enemies by embracing them as friends. By praying for them. Blessing them. Loving them. Love your enemies? Are you serious?

The second counterintuitive proposition was that the Kingdom would find its ultimate demonstration of power through the death of its king. Rather than requiring Jesus' followers to die for him, Jesus submitted himself to be put to death as a picture of sacrificial love. I can hear his followers saying, "Now wait a minute. You are the leader of this revolutionary movement, and you're going to die at the hands of our enemies?"

Gregory Boyd, Pastor of Woodland Hills Church in Minneapolis, often speaks on what he calls "Christus Victor" to emphasize why Jesus had to die. He says the death of Jesus is an ultimate conquest over evil and its powers. Jesus' entire time here was pushing back the kingdom of evil. This is why Jesus broke the religious and cultural taboos, why he broke religious traditions, healing and feeding people on the Sabbath, why he touched the untouchables, why he crossed the racial and gender lines, why he showed mercy to the condemned people, why he lifted up the children, why he, the master, became the servant to wash the disciples' feet—because everything about Jesus' life was an act of self-sacrificial love. The Kingdom Jesus was promoting was the fountain of this kind of love that flows with peace, joy, and reconciliation. Jesus' death defeats all of the self-centered gods of this world.

Today, no one is a follower of a Roman emperor.

Yet Jesus is followed by millions throughout the world.

Today, the Roman Empire doesn't even exist.

Yet the Kingdom of God is everywhere.

So, who won?

Jesus Shifts from Miracles to Parables

In the Spirit fully embodying the Kingdom on earth and bringing freedom to all he encountered, Jesus heals a man who was demonized in such a way that the man could not see nor speak. Since this was one of the miracles the people thought the Messiah would perform, this was too threatening for those in power within the Jewish leadership. When Jesus performed this incredible miracle, the Pharisees and the leadership attributed this work to the devil—Beelzebub (Matthew 12).

With this widespread rejection of Jesus, the disciples had to be very discouraged and their hopes dashed. The disciples had been riding high, following and promoting their "candidate" for the new leader of the Jews who would surely put an end to the Roman domination. His popularity was skyrocketing, until now.

With this in mind, a question the disciples (the many followers of Jesus, not just the twelve) must have asked of Jesus: "What's the Kingdom going to look like now?" In order to communicate the principles of the Kingdom, Jesus shifts into a new form of teaching. The method is called parables or visual stories.

Everyone noticed the difference in Jesus' approach and the disciples asked about it. The disciples came to him and asked, "Why do you speak to the people in parables?" He replied, "The knowledge of the secrets of the kingdom of heaven has been given to you, but not to them. Those who have will be given more, and they will have an abundance. As for those who do not have, even what they have will be taken from them. This is why I speak to them in parables: "Though seeing, they do not see; though hearing, they do not hear or understand. In them is fulfilled the prophecy of Isaiah: 'You will be ever hearing but never understanding; you will be ever seeing but never perceiving. For this people's heart has become calloused; they hardly hear with their ears, and they have closed their eyes. Otherwise they might see with their eyes, hear with their ears, understand with their hearts and turn, and I would heal them.'

"But blessed are your eyes because they see, and your ears because they hear. Truly I tell you, many prophets and righteous people longed to see what you see but did not see it, and to hear what you hear but did not hear it" (Matthew

13).

Jesus revealed two purposes for shifting into teaching in parables. Jesus wanted his disciples to know about the Kingdom, because they had ears to hear and eyes to see. In other words, they were leaning in and interested. The other purpose was to conceal these principles from those who weren't interested or leaning in—those who didn't have eyes to see or ears to hear. In a way, this was a very compassionate thing for Jesus to do. To continue to heap truth on those who were already rejecting it was to heap up more and more condemnation on these people. This takes us back to a most basic principle that God only requires that we be interested and lean in, then we will see and hear more.

Parable of the Soils

Matthew records eight parables at the beginning of this shift in Jesus' manner of teaching. Jesus sets the tone of his parabolic teaching with the parable of the soils: "A farmer went out to sow his seed. As he was scattering the seed, some fell along the path, and the birds came and ate it up. Some fell on rocky places, where it did not have much soil. It sprang up quickly, because the soil was shallow. But when the sun came up, the plants were scorched, and they withered because they had no root. Other seed fell among thorns, which grew up and choked the plants. Still other seed fell on good soil, where it produced a crop—a hundred, sixty or thirty times what was sown. Whoever has ears, let them hear" (Matthew 13).

Next, Jesus explains this parable: "Listen then to what the parable of the sower means: When people hear the message about the kingdom and do not understand it, the evil one comes and snatches away what was sown in their hearts. This is the seed sown along the path. The seed falling on rocky ground refers to people who hear the word and at once receive it with joy. But since they have no root, they last only a short time. When trouble or persecution comes because of the word, they quickly fall away. The seed falling among the thorns refers to people who hear the word, but the worries of this life and the deceitfulness of wealth choke the word, making it unfruitful. But the seed falling on good soil refers to people who hear the word and understand it. They produce a crop, yielding a hundred, sixty, or thirty times what was sown" (Matthew 13).

This parable is popularly called the "parable of the sower," yet it is really all about the soils and how the soils respond to the seed sown. A healthy and receptive soil to a seed planted will establish a root, produce a shoot, and then the fruit will emerge. Soil along the path cannot receive the seed planted, because it's too hard and the seeds are snatched away. Jesus' point is that this soil doesn't have ears to hear or eyes to see at all.

The rocky soil receives the seed, but cannot establish a root. This kind of soil represents a person who initially hears and sees, but is discouraged by trials and persecution—hard times.

The thorny soil is initially receptive—ears to hear and eyes to see, but the seed is choked by the worries of this life and the deceitfulness of riches.

Jesus then speaks of the good soil—the person who is completely receptive to the seed and prepared for growth. This is truly the person Jesus is always looking for—those with ears to hear and eyes to see.

Note a few observations on this parable: in Matthew's version of this teaching Jesus says that he is the sower. When Jesus was physically on the earth, his words were pitched out to those who listened to him. Today, Jesus is still sowing the seed, but now he is doing it through our lives and through the stories of those who are following him.

Sowing seed during that time was not like taking a

package of seed and carefully putting them in the ground. It was a scattering method, usually throwing it out by hand. Therefore the sowing was indiscriminate and the seed was in essence planted everywhere. This is why some seed lands in the different places—beside the road, on rocky places, among the thorns, and upon the good soil.

Jesus refers to the seed sown in three ways (Matthew 13; Luke 8): The seed is the "word of God." The seed is the "message of the Kingdom." The seed is the "sons of the Kingdom."

Jesus seems to view the seed sown in and through the sons of the Kingdom as the word of God and the message of God's Kingdom. This is what his primary message was as he taught throughout the villages and synagogues. *Therefore, the word of God—the message of the Kingdom—is the active presence of God, working within, among, and through the followers of Jesus in the form of a seed.*

This seed has tremendous spiritual power within those who are followers of Jesus—to be productive—to be fruitful. It is able to produce amazing levels of fruit. To be fruitful is to enjoy the peace, joy, love, and grace of Jesus for yourself and if you as a follower show up, you can bring that same fruit for those in need.

Its effect on you and through you is determined by your response to the seed. It's all a matter of responsiveness. Note that you are not responsible to bring forth the fruit, but the power of the seed will produce the fruit if planted in the good soil. I've come to realize that these soils are dynamic in our lives. I have been each of these soils at one time or another. Can you see this in your life as well?

This answers what I see with people who seem to "get it," yet fade away. This also answers what I see with people who all of a sudden "get it," yet they have been around this sowing for years. Now, here is what impresses me most about this teaching. Jesus is saying that if you have ears to hear and eyes to see, you are receptive to the Good News of the Kingdom. And in this receptive mode, Jesus measures the fruitfulness. He uses 30, 60, and 100 fold to measure fruitfulness! Fruitfulness is basically the spiritual growth and maturity in your own life and the effects of your life on others around you. He begins with 30 fold. To be 30 fold is multiplied by 30 times that of a normal crop. So, this means that the lowest level of fruitfulness will be outstanding. Then, He goes on to say you may enjoy multiples of that, even to the point of 60 and 100 fold. That's incredible—beyond belief!

Out of all of the eight parables recorded in Matthew 13 only one parable has an action step to it. There is one primary activity within the Kingdom Jesus came to establish. It's right here in the parable of the soils. The primary activity of the Kingdom is the constant sowing of the seed of the Good News of the Kingdom.

Please note: the primary activity is *not* trying to get people to go to heaven.

It is *not* trying to convert people to join a certain religion.

It is *not* trying to get people to join your religious organization.

The primary activity is the sowing of seed—introducing the Word of God, the Good News of the Kingdom, which is present and alive within and among the followers of Jesus. The primary activity is introducing people to the person of Jesus—without all the religious baggage.

After the parable of the soils, Jesus introduces seven additional parables. Each one is more descriptive of what "the Kingdom is like" and offers a picture of the nature of the Kingdom of God on earth.

Remember, all of the parables are presented to answer the question in the minds of his disciples, "What's the Kingdom going to look like, now that the Jewish leadership has totally rejected Jesus as God's Messiah?" Each parable is a description of the Kingdom that Jesus came to establish.

Parable of the Weeds

"The kingdom of heaven is like a man who sowed good seed in his field. But while everyone was sleeping, his enemy came and sowed weeds (tares) among the wheat, and went away. When the wheat sprouted and formed heads, then the weeds also appeared. The owner's servants came to him and said, 'Sir, didn't you sow good seed in your field? Where then did the weeds come from?'

"'An enemy did this,' he replied. The servants asked him, 'Do you want us to go and pull them up?' 'No,' he answered, 'because while you are pulling the weeds, you may uproot the wheat with them. Let both grow together until the harvest. At that time I will tell the harvesters: 'First collect the weeds and tie them in bundles to be burned; then gather the wheat and bring it into my barn'"(Matthew 13).

Jesus says that there will be genuine wheat and weeds growing side by side in the Kingdom. The Kingdom consists of the weeds (the bad seed) growing alongside the genuine wheat (the good seed). When one is caught up in the work of sowing, there will likely be a discovery of weeds (tares) that are sown along side the wheat. These tares are empty wheat pods—chaff without wheat kernels—false wheat that looks like wheat, but isn't. The genuine wheat plants are those who believe in the Gospel of the Kingdom and the tares or weeds are those who look good, but are not genuine followers of Jesus. They are all together in the same field and it may be difficult to tell the difference.

The servants' tendency is to want to remove the tares out of the wheat field—to separate the wheat from the weeds. But the owner quickly responds, "Allow both to grow together until the harvest." The reason being that if one attempts to pull out the weeds from the wheat, there's a great likelihood that the genuine wheat will also be pulled out. In other words, it is none of our business who is *in* and who is *out*.

Only Jesus knows for sure!

Parable of the Mustard Seed

Jesus continues: "The kingdom of heaven is like a mustard seed, which a man took and planted in his field. Though it is the smallest of all seeds, yet when it grows, it is the largest of garden plants and becomes a tree, so that the birds come and perch in its branches" (Matthew 13).

The mustard seed is among the smallest of the seeds and has the ability to grow into a tree that is large enough for birds to perch. Jesus is saying here that the Kingdom will experience incredible growth. It may seem very small and insignificant at the beginning, yet will most surely grow immensely. You can count on that and be encouraged by it. No church, mosque, or temple can count on this kind of growth. The Kingdom of God can!

Another way to look at this is that the Kingdom is a completely different thing. The Kingdom is invisible. Because you can't see it, you don't expect a massive growth, but it occurs silently and pervasively. The Kingdom can penetrate any culture and supersedes any organization, no matter how large or active it may be. The Kingdom's incredible growth can only be explained by the power of God. No man-made program can do any better. No man-made program has *ever* done any better. This is a vital secret of the Kingdom that Jesus reveals here.

Parable of the Leaven

"The kingdom of heaven is like yeast that a woman took and mixed into about sixty pounds of flour until it worked all through the dough" (Matthew 13).

Once the leaven or yeast is introduced into the

dough, it spreads everywhere throughout the whole lump. What's interesting is that it cannot be stopped. Once it is introduced, it cannot be removed. So, the teaching here is Kingdom growth will be irreversible, once introduced into a person, a community, a society, and a nation. Nothing will be able to stop it. Nothing and no one can stop it from spreading—not communism, fascism, racism, or any other isms. When the Kingdom spreads, it supersedes all sorts of movements and organizations. This is why to follow Jesus most effectively, it's important to be a Kingdom person first and foremost.

To be anything else is to be so much less!

You know what's interesting? The movement of the Kingdom is going on, no matter what you or I think, say, or do. Our primary responsibility is not to make something happen, but to see where Jesus is at work and go there to join him in the work already in progress. The movement of Jesus and the Kingdom is already in motion. The question is whether or not you will join it or start your own. Remember, it's irreversible! It cannot be stopped.

Parable of the Hidden Treasure and Parable of the Pearl

"The kingdom of heaven is like treasure hidden in a field. When a man found it, he hid it again, and then in his joy went and sold all he had and bought that field. Again, the kingdom of heaven is like a merchant looking for fine pearls. When he found one of great value, he went away and sold everything he had and bought it" (Matthew 13).

These two parables are similar, but, at the same time, different.

The similarity between the two seems to be this: when a person hears the message of the Kingdom and receives it, he becomes convinced the Kingdom is the most valuable thing he's ever heard before. Therefore he is willing to sell everything to possess it.

The difference between the two seems to be this: the man who finds the hidden treasure in the field, hides it again, and sells all he has to buy that field is a person who comes into the Kingdom *by surprise*. He is so filled with joy, because he wasn't even looking for it. I have several friends who are still shocked they are walking with Jesus in the Kingdom today. The man who is the merchant looking for fine pearls, finds the best one ever and sells everything he has to buy that pearl. He is the person who comes into the Kingdom *by searching*, knowing its value. So, people will come into the Kingdom in all sorts of ways, but ultimately either by searching or surprise.

Do you know people who are like these two? The one who by surprise discovers the Kingdom treasures—the one who would never be "caught dead" sitting among a group of Jesus followers? This person, along with many onlookers, is quite surprised that he found such a valuable thing. Or the one who by searching out truth or the meaning of life or whatever, finds himself delighted to have found a satisfaction that no one can take away, so he sold everything he had in order to own it.

Note that both have the same response. They each sell all they have and buy their newfound treasure. This has nothing to do with purchasing or performing well enough to gain a place in the Kingdom. But it has everything to do with the comparable value of being with the King in the Kingdom rather than going through the motions, living a life that is routine and predictable with all of the traditional comforts of life—all without the King and outside the realm of his Kingdom. So, how do you value your relationship with the King and his Kingdom?

Is it the most valuable, priceless, place to be, ever?

Or is it just a pleasant place to visit from time to time?

This is the difference between being a spectator and

a participant!

Parable of the Net

"Once again, the kingdom of heaven is like a net that was let down into the lake and caught all kinds of fish. When it was full, the fishermen pulled it up on the shore. Then they sat down and collected the good fish in baskets, but threw the bad away. This is how it will be at the end of the age. The angels will come and separate the wicked from the righteous and throw them into the blazing furnace, where there will be weeping and gnashing of teeth" (Matthew 13).

Whatever else the net means, Jesus wants to make certain his disciples understand that there will be a sorting and that he will be in charge of it. His disciples don't have to do any sorting whatsoever. In fact, it's clear that no follower of Jesus can do anything with respect to the ultimate results of who are the wicked and who are the righteous.

Note the term "wicked" that Jesus frequently uses. He isn't speaking of a vile, despicable person, but "wicked" is used of those who do not hear or welcome the words of Jesus and do not practice them.

The primary issue here for me is that the parable of the net teaches us that there will be an accounting at the end. And that everyone will be caught in the net for the final accounting.

Parable of the Scribe

"Therefore every teacher of the law who has been instructed about the kingdom of heaven is like the owner of a house who brings out of his storeroom new treasures as well as old."

This is the last of the eight parables in Matthew 13, a parable that has been so easily overlooked. I've overlooked it until recently.

Jesus is referring to a person who is a teacher of the Law—one who knows the Law well. Then, this one who is conversant with the Law is taught the message of the Kingdom of heaven. A person in this position is like the owner of a house who is able to share with his guests new things (things of the Kingdom) as well as the old things (the Law). In fact, what we're discovering is that walking with Jesus in the Kingdom lifestyle brings something new and fresh every day. Personally, my learning curve isn't a curve anymore; it's perpendicular! It's the most thrilling adventure ever!

As Jesus makes the shift into teaching by way of parables, he lays a foundation for understanding the Kingdom principles for those who have ears to hear and eyes to see. Several helpful factors stand out: The most powerful element of the Kingdom lifestyle exists in a seed, and a very small one at that. Therefore the power of the Kingdom is not what is readily seen. It's invisible, imperceptible, and yet indelible in its markings on those who follow after Jesus and those they touch.

The second most important element of this Kingdom lifestyle is that it requires each follower to prepare his or her heart to receive the seed in order to establish its root, develop a shoot and bear fruit. Even as I say that, I realize that preparation of the heart may be more what you don't do, than what you do.

That you *don't* allow the trials and troubles which come against you to distract you away from having a receptive heart—that is leaning into the ways of Jesus and the Kingdom.

That you *don't* get caught up in worrying about your life and your world.

That you *don't* allow the riches of this world to deceive you into thinking they are more important than walking in the ways of Jesus and the Kingdom lifestyle.

If you *don't* do these things, you will be able to keep

your soil good and receptive to the seed of the Word of God—the message of the Kingdom.

Jesus revealed the secrets of the Kingdom—the secrets to living life most fully with him and his principles. Jesus revealed the mystery of the Kingdom lifestyle. Remember, the principles of the Kingdom are actually the principles of life. Jesus' teachings are primarily about the Kingdom way of life. If you get into the flow of the Kingdom way of life, you will experience the greatest personal and relational satisfaction possible, no matter what comes your way.

This is not only the *right* way to live your life; it's the *best* way!

More importantly, it is Jesus' way.

He plants a seed in the soil of your heart. Then he waits. Knowing that in time the seed will germinate, take root, and eventually transform you.

From the inside out!

This is the essence of the secrets that Jesus reveals.

Part IV

the power of the few

CHAPTER 11

Was the Cross the Finished Work of Jesus?

The three essentials to *Jesus Plus Nothing* are:

- The pre-eminence of Jesus—making the main thing the main thing!

- The presence of the Kingdom—embracing the principles of Jesus as a lifestyle!

- The power of the few!

The first two essentials are most effectively activated in the power of the few. This may be the most counterintuitive dimension within the Jesus movement. "The power of the few" contains the same core idea as the seed. Just as the seed is small and seemingly insignificant, proving to become large, irreversible in its growth, and powerful enough to accomplish inner transformation, so it is with the power of the few.

The Model of Jesus

The primary example of the "power of the few" is found in Jesus' method of operation. Instead of using "Madison Avenue" marketing methods, Jesus launched his movement with a few—just three to be exact—Peter, James, and John. He then selected nine more. After that he sent out 72 in pairs to carry the message of the Kingdom. Although Jesus spoke to large groups from time to time, he mostly hung out with a few at a time. Jesus knew by working with a few who really "get it," the power of that few would be revolutionary!

The Mode of the Disciples

Jesus was the model. The disciples of Jesus learned to follow the model that was set. They always traveled and ministered in teams of two or more. They practiced the power of the few very effectively. They even authored several of the books of the New Testament, often in tandem with others. For instance, the first letter to the Corinthians (1 Corinthians) is attributed to Paul. But Paul didn't write the letter to the community of believers in Corinth, alone. Right up front within the letter it says Paul *and* Sosthenes were the authors. This may be the same Sosthenes who was the leader of the synagogue in Corinth. Paul had help writing the second letter to the Corinthians, too. Paul and Timothy wrote that letter. Timothy also co-authored Philippians, Colossians, and Philemon with him. The letter to the gathering of Jesus' followers in Galatia is said to be written by Paul and "all the brothers and sisters with me." Then, in the book of 1 John, John says that "which we have heard, which we have seen with our eyes, which we have looked at and our hands have touched . . . this we proclaim concerning the Word of life." Note that this letter was composed by a group of people that John called "we."

The Blueprint for Worldwide Revolution

Read the book of 1 Thessalonians and you will discover that even though Paul is again listed as the author, yet this isn't exactly true. I first saw this through a brother and friend, and now I have asked a question over and over to pastors, professors, counselors, Bible students, and to hundreds of people at gatherings. The question is simple. After having them silently read the first chapter of the book of 1 Thessalonians, I ask, "Who wrote 1 Thessalonians?" No one has given me the correct answer yet. Most everyone answers, "Paul!" I did the same thing when I was asked. However, in the very first verse it clearly says who wrote it. It was Paul, Silvanus (Silas), and Timothy. These three wrote the book. And it was the dynamic relationship of these three men that the Thessalonians imitated. These three men practiced the principle of the power of the few and their work proved to be most effective and most powerful.

Their ministry followed Jesus' pattern of walking together as a few and echoed forth from the believers in Thessalonica throughout Greece and much of the rest of the world. The Thessalonians were known for their faith that worked (work of faith), their love that worked (labor of love), and their hope that persevered (steadfastness of hope). The citizens of Thessalonica saw something so unique it persuaded them to turn to God from idols to serve the living and true God and to wait for Jesus to return.

The most shocking thing about their response is how it all began. The history of Paul, Silas, and Timothy's work among the Thessalonians is recorded in Acts 17. These three men in fellowship with one another, walking with Jesus and with one another, were putting into practice the promise that Jesus had given them: "Where two or three are gathered together, there I will be in their midst." When these three men walked together in Jesus, he showed up powerfully. They were practicing the power of the few. They really got it, and it was so evident that it spread contagiously.

An explosion occurred in the hearts of many in Thessalonica that was inspired by the personal transforming power of Jesus seen in these three men. This is what is termed the "spontaneous expansion" of the community of Jesus. And this explosion spread like wildfire. Note that the "spontaneous expansion" of the Jesus community was spread by word of mouth—no TV or radio broadcasts, no podcasts, no internet, no sermons on CDs. By the way, this is the same today. The best way to spread the message of Jesus and the Kingdom is by word of mouth—a life-on-life experience through a few that "get it."

When Paul, Silas, and Timothy entered into the city of Thessalonica, they met all sorts of people with a variety of gods and their corresponding idols. They stuck to their message of Jesus and the Kingdom and experienced an amazing response. That response spread throughout Asia Minor. The Good News of Jesus and the Kingdom is spread through a few who have been transformed by the power of Jesus.

Not only did Jesus and his followers use the power of the few most effectively, but today those who follow Jesus follow that same pattern. The power of the few is what many have always sought within the organized Church when they feel the need to promote small groups of any kind. But even a small group may not get the results that we're talking about in the "power of the few." The real dynamic of the "power of the few" is genuine fellowship—participation in one another's lives in such a way so as to develop a personal support system. This support system becomes so strengthening that it serves as an inner security system. I am stronger as I live my life in relationship with other brothers and sisters who are followers of Jesus.

In the past, I've spent so much energy producing the best possible speeches to the masses. However, I always knew that there were some universal principles at play in that sort of venue. Upon hearing me speak, only 5% really get it, 15% think they get it, and 80% remain somewhere in the fog with no idea what was said. Oh, they will remember an illustration or two or a joke or two, but they will likely miss the essential point of the message. Now that I am into the power of the few, I am discovering that the few really do get it and embrace it for themselves. You see, when someone really gets what it means to walk with Jesus in his

Kingdom presence, the message becomes contagious. To me, the power of the few is a must for all who are serious about following Jesus, *simply* Jesus.

The understanding of the power of the few emanates from more than anecdotal observations. According to Jesus, it is irrefutably tied to the work his Father sent him to do.

"It Is Finished"

When Jesus was nailed to the cross, he spoke seven times. One of these sayings of Jesus was "It is finished." If you were to survey most people who have seriously read the Bible today and ask them what was the "finished work" of Jesus or what Jesus came to accomplish, you will receive the same answer most every time. To most, the "finished work" of Jesus was to die on the cross for the sins of the world. Jesus did come to die and he mentioned this a few times with his disciples. Although this does seem to be the logical answer to "what is the finished work of Jesus?", Jesus specifically tells us otherwise.

It is true that when Jesus said these words, it marked the finished work of the Christ on the cross. He had finished the sacrifice that was required for the redemption of the world.

However, a few days before Jesus died on the cross, he revealed what his "finished work" actually was—the reason why he was sent here. So, what did Jesus say was the work he came to complete? What was it that Jesus came to do? It's within these words of Jesus' prayer in John 17 that we find the true revolutionary nature of what Jesus came to do and what he expects from his followers. Jesus said that he finished the work the Father sent him to do: "I have brought you glory on earth by finishing the work you gave me to do." Once you embrace what Jesus says was his finished work, the work he came to accomplish, it will change what you're doing with your life.

A clue?

It's all about the power of the few.

The Finished Work of Jesus

At the close of Jesus' work with his disciples, Jesus prays earnestly to his Father. Jesus prays concerning himself. Jesus prays concerning his early disciples. Jesus prays concerning all those who will become his followers in the future. It's within this prayer that Jesus seems to unveil the original plan behind "the power of the few." What makes "the power of the few" so revolutionary is that working with the few is the unlikely key to reaching the masses, because working with a few who really get it is life-changing for the few and the many.

Check out what Jesus says about his "finished work" in his prayer: "This is eternal life, that they may know You, the only true God, and Jesus the Christ whom You have sent. I glorified You on the earth, having accomplished the work which You have given me to do. I have manifested Your name to the men whom You gave me out of the world; they were Yours and You gave them to me, and they have kept Your word.

"Now they have come to know that everything You have given me is from You; for the words which You gave me I have given to them; and they received them and truly understood that I came forth from You, and they believed that You sent me.

". . . And I come to You, Holy Father, keep them in Your name, the name which You have given me, that they may be one even as we are. While I was with them, I was keeping them in Your name which You have given me. . . . But now I come to You; and these things I speak in the world so that they may have my joy made full in themselves. I have given them Your word . . . . Sanctify (set apart) them in the truth; Your word is truth. As You sent me into the world, I also have sent them into the world.

"I do not ask on behalf of these alone, but for those also who believe in me through their word; that they may all be one; even as You, Father, are in me and I in You, that they also may be in Us, so that the world may believe that You sent me. The glory which You have given me I have given to them, that they may be one, just as We are one; I in them and You in me, that they may be perfected in unity, so that the world may know that You sent me, and loved them, even as You have loved Me.

"O righteous Father, although the world has not known You, yet I have known You; and these have known that You sent me; and I have made Your name known to them, and will make it known, so that the love with which You loved me may be in them, and I in them" (John 17).

There are several things that stand out to me here from the specific words of Jesus recorded in John 17. The revolutionary work Jesus came to accomplish—the finished work—was to share with his disciples certain words from the Father. Wow, if we only knew what these "words" were that the Father gave Jesus to share with the disciples, we could continue this as the work Jesus is still accomplishing today. Well, I think we do know what those words are, certainly for the most part. These words are recorded for us in the five Gospels—Matthew, Mark, Luke, John, and Acts. So, maybe it makes sense to focus most of our energies in learning what Jesus shared with his disciples in order to embrace the revolutionary work of Jesus.

The revolutionary work Jesus came to accomplish was to be done with a few. I am continually struck with this fact. Jesus, in his infinite wisdom, saw that it would be most effective to work with a few as he shared what the Father sent him to share. He was not tempted to share it with the masses, because he knew that they wouldn't "get it." In fact, it took a long time for the few to "get it."

175

By going to the masses, Jesus would have produced hearers of the word who deceive themselves, rather than doers of the word. Think about it. Most life-changing experiences (truly transformational experiences) in your life have come in relationship with a few. So, if that is true (and I'm convinced it is), why aren't we more compelled to share with others in such a way so they can have the same transformational experience? The "power of the few" or the context of community is necessary for people to experience authentic transformation as they follow Jesus.

The revolutionary work Jesus came to accomplish was to be different from the world system already in place. Jesus, as the King of kings, came to establish his Kingdom on earth with those who become his disciples on the earth. This Kingdom is not separate from the earth, but different from it. Check it out. What Jesus shared seems to most always be just the opposite of what the world system is today and just the opposite of what we feel is the natural thing to do. Instead of buying and selling being the primary theme, Jesus teaches giving and receiving. Instead of getting even, Jesus teaches the supernatural power of forgiveness. Instead of avoiding pain and suffering, Jesus teaches to embrace your pain and suffering so that you will emerge more whole. Instead of being repulsed by the poor, diseased, and disabled, Jesus teaches to go to them and extend his love toward them. Instead of going with the crowd, Jesus teaches us to stand with him and his people. Instead of loving the masses in general (whatever that means), Jesus teaches us to love one another—on a personal level.

Note something even more significant than the teachings of Jesus. Jesus didn't just teach these dynamic principles and thoughts; he lived them out. He forgave, he healed, he touched, and he hurt with those in need.

The revolutionary work Jesus came to accomplish was to be passed on by his disciples to others over the generations to come. Jesus came to share these "words" from the

Father to those who will share these "words" with others. He even prays for those who will believe through these first few for generations to come. It's just that simple. The message of Jesus is fully expressed when one learns to pass it on. To put it another way: the one who teaches another learns twice!

The revolutionary work Jesus came to accomplish will result in his disciples having his joy made full in them and being loved the same way the Father loved Jesus—all wrapped up in one another in a unique oneness with the Father, Jesus, and the disciples. This makes it all worth being a revolutionary with Jesus. You will know what it means to have his full joy and you will be enveloped in his love and the love of the Father. Possessing these two results will encourage you to continue, allowing Jesus' finished work to work itself out through you.

I have known this joy and this love from time to time in my life, but not on a continual basis . . . until Jesus apprehended my life in a new and very real way. This is what makes this life of practicing Kingdom principles and acting as revolutionaries in the name of Jesus such an enjoyable adventure.

The revolutionary work Jesus came to accomplish is not limited to the first 12 apostles/disciples, but is for those of us who are his followers today. This is not another good Bible story to be filed away for small group discussions later. This is crucial for our lives today! But let me take the edge off a bit by saying that being a revolutionary on your own or with a group of people has nothing to do with you and your performance. Being a revolutionary is simply lifting Jesus up in your life and inviting him to do his revolutionary work in you and through you as you touch others. It has nothing to do with "converting" people to a group, a club, a church, or a religious system, but it is all about transformation. This is why I've always said that the Reformation never went far enough. We must never settle for anything less than transformation and the only person I've ever seen who can accomplish transformation, changing a person's heart inside out, is Jesus. Consider joining the revolution, because the revolution is still on and thriving all over the planet!

The Key to the Finished Work of Jesus

Jesus' finished work has an additional element that you might overlook. Jesus didn't come just to receive and empower the few disciples God sent. He didn't come to work with a few individuals. Jesus came to invite these few individuals into the dynamic of fellowship. Fellowship with Jesus and one another is the key to Jesus' finished work.

Walking together is practicing the presence of the Kingdom. Practicing the presence of the Kingdom requires fellowship. The term fellowship is widely known, but even more widely misunderstood. It's more than a "potluck" dinner. It's not a room called the "fellowship hall". It's more than a group of friends watching football or hunting together. The fellowship may be the most important concept you will ever learn. However, this concept is not just to be learned; it begs to be lived!

Jesus' strategic approach to spreading his Good News message throughout the world never involved "putting up another church," but practicing church. He taught his followers not to build the church, but to be the church. This is what the fellowship is all about!

The fellowship is the answer to becoming the genuine salt and light that Jesus intended his followers to be. My friend who challenged me to be more strategic with my life also painted a couple of vivid pictures that are now etched in my mind indelibly. He urged me to be a fountain. "You don't take the fountain to people; the people come to the fountain" he said. "In the same way, you are to be a light that attracts. Just as bugs are attracted to physical light, people are attracted to spiritual light. So be a light! Be a beacon! If Jesus is lifted up, he will draw all men unto him." The fellowship operates on the principle of attraction, not promotion. This goes against the grain of most every religious program in our world.

Fellowship is best understood as a verb! The fellowship is not an organization, an institution, or a denomination. Fellowship is a verb that, when properly activated, has the power to change the world—one person at a time!

The primary term for fellowship in the New Testament is *koinonia*. The word has the idea of communion or sharing in common with another. It's the perfect word to describe the relationship we are to have with God and with one another—a partnership.

There are three dynamic Greek words with a message of encouragement that can help you to stay on track with Jesus and to participate in a revolutionary fellowship that can transform the world.

Parakoloutheo—Keep on committing yourself to follow closely after one another. It means "to follow close up, or side by side," or "to accompany, to conform to" or "follow" teaching so that you practice it. There is a sense of following so closely that you can more fully know a person or persons.

Katartizo—Keep on restoring one another (the true revolution). It is used in several ways in the New Testament: to restore, to perfect, to fit, to prepare, etc. Possibly the most interesting use of the word is "to mend" a net. Fishermen around the world spend as much of their time mending nets as they do fishing. The maintenance of close relationships requires our attention to mending as well. It's even used for a physician to reset broken bones. So, this word has three basic meanings: to mend or repair the nets. To complete, furnish completely, to equip or to prepare. To prepare and perfect ethically and spiritually.

Haplotes—Keep on reminding one another of the

simplicity of Jesus. This is a fascinating word that has more to it than simply simplicity. This simplicity carries with it sincerity, single-mindedness, and genuineness. There is also a notion of generosity and bountifulness in this simplicity. In other words, the simplicity of devotion to Jesus has a single-minded abundance to it—an overflowing fullness and liberality about it.

The Kingdom Jesus intended has to do with experiencing a revolutionary fellowship with Jesus and those who are also following him. Although this isn't the primary purpose of a weekend big C Church service due to the nature of its size, you can experience a revolutionary fellowship within the big C Church in smaller settings.

The power of the few is the best place to experience the pre-eminence of Jesus and the presence of the Kingdom. I've always taught that Jesus is pre-eminent—that he is awesome, but I've never experienced Jesus in this way until I started practicing the power of the few.

Jesus said that where two or three are gathered together, he will show up. The power of the few is the dwelling place of the presence of Jesus, himself. Now, if you were convinced that Jesus was going to show up some place, wouldn't you go and make yourself available to see him as quickly as possible? Do whatever you can do to participate in the power of the few.

The power of the few is at the core of what Jesus came to accomplish—to pour his life and energy into those few God sent his way. A good way to test out how you are practicing the power of the few is to ask yourself three questions:

- Who are the few God has sent your way?

- What are you teaching them?

- What are they teaching you?

CHAPTER 12

When Does Jesus Show Up and What Happens When He Does?

Jesus shows up "where two or three come together in his name." When he does show up, no one is the same again. The dead are brought back to life. The blind see. The lame walk. The deaf hear. The mute talk. Enemies and rivals become friends. The status of women is elevated. The poor are made rich. The rich realize their poverty. The lost are found. The weak find strength. The strong are made aware of weakness.

No transformation is more vivid than what happened to the early disciples. Most were weak-willed and timid; they eventually found inner strength and courage. The usual reason given for this dramatic life-change is the resurrection of Jesus from the dead. The resurrection is no doubt paramount, however I see their transformation coming from something else. As mentioned earlier, after the resurrection, it is recorded that Jesus spent 40 days with the disciples, where he spoke to them about the Kingdom of God.

Check out what Peter shared regarding that time, when he spoke to those gathered in the house of Cornelius: "We are witnesses of everything he did in the country of the Jews and in Jerusalem. They killed him by hanging him on a cross, but God raised him from the dead on the third day and caused him to be seen. He was not seen by all the people, but by witnesses whom God had already chosen—*by us who ate and drank with him after he rose from the dead.* He commanded us to preach to the people and to testify that he is the one whom God appointed as judge of the living and the dead. All the prophets testify about him that everyone who believes in him receives forgiveness of sins through his name" (Acts 10).

I think the real transformation the disciples experienced took place during this time spent with Jesus, eating and drinking and discussing principles of the Kingdom of God. The same thing happens today. When two or three are gathered together in the name of Jesus, he will show up and make a significant difference in all who experience him.

Diana and I have the privilege of gathering together with a few followers of Jesus. We've been meeting with one group of followers weekly for several years. Week after week as we are doing life together, we have faced nearly every kind of pain, disease, and loss imaginable. We turn every problem over to the care and direction of Jesus. When we need healing, we ask for Jesus to come through on our behalf. When we have financial needs, we ask for his help. When we need wisdom for decision-making, we count on his wisdom. When we are grieving a loss of a loved one, we count on his peace. When we seek answers from Jesus, we have found that he shows up.

Here is my point: if Jesus brings positive transformation into every life he encounters, then doesn't it make sense for us to introduce Jesus to everyone who is interested? You see, when Jesus shows up, no one is ever the same again!

When Jesus Showed Up in the Area of Capernaum

There are many stories of Jesus encounters, but two of my favorites illustrate him at his very best. The first is when he touched two unclean women, breaking all the rules, traditions, and customs of the day. This story is recorded in the fifth chapter of the Gospel of Mark:

"When Jesus had again crossed over by boat to the other side of the lake, a large crowd gathered around him while he was by the lake. Then one of the synagogue leaders, named Jairus, came, and when he saw Jesus, he fell at his feet. He pleaded earnestly with him, 'My little daughter is dying. Please come and put your hands on her so that she will be healed and live.' So Jesus went with him.

"A large crowd followed and pressed around him. And a woman was there who had been subject to bleeding for twelve years. She had suffered a great deal under the care of many doctors and had spent all she had, yet instead of getting better she grew worse. When she heard about Jesus, she came up behind him in the crowd and touched his cloak, because she thought, 'If I just touch his clothes, I will be healed.' Immediately her bleeding stopped and she felt in her body that she was freed from her suffering. At once Jesus realized that power had gone out from him. He turned around in the crowd and asked, 'Who touched my clothes?' 'You see the people crowding against you,' his disciples answered, 'and yet you can ask, 'Who touched me?' But Jesus kept looking around to see who had done it. Then the woman, knowing what had happened to her, came and fell at his feet and, trembling with fear, told him the whole truth. He said to her, 'Daughter, your faith has healed you. Go in peace and be freed from your suffering.'

"While Jesus was still speaking, some people came from the house of Jairus, the synagogue leader. 'Your daughter is dead,' they said. 'Why bother the teacher anymore?' Overhearing what they said, Jesus told him, 'Don't be afraid; just believe.'

"He did not let anyone follow him except Peter, James, and John, the brother of James. When they came to the home of the synagogue leader, Jesus saw a commotion, with people crying and wailing loudly. He went in and said to them, 'Why all this commotion and wailing? The child is not dead but asleep.' But the crowd laughed at him.

"After Jesus put them all out, he took the child's father and mother and the disciples who were with him, and went in where the child was. He took her by the hand and said to her, 'Little girl, I say to you, get up!' Immediately the girl stood up and began to walk around (she was twelve years old). At this they were completely astonished. He gave strict orders not to let anyone know about this, and told them to give her something to eat" (Mark 5).

This is a fascinating story where Jesus was on his way to perform a miracle and stopped for another divine appointment. These two stories fused together are interesting to compare. Both women are called daughters, one by the father and one by Jesus. Both have to do with the number 12—the age of Jairus' daughter and the number of years of suffering of the woman—and in both situations faith was key. Jairus and the woman both saw Jesus as the only answer to their need.

There was a superstition at that time that seems to have motivated the woman to touch Jesus' garments. The fringe worn on the border of the outer garment was believed to have special power of the Messiah's robe. If she could just touch that fringe border, then she might be healed of her condition.

Jesus shows himself to be the physician and healer of the unacceptable and the sick, when he healed this woman. Think of her desperation. She had been ceremonially unclean because of her bleeding for 12 years. That adds up to 12 years of disappointment, 12 years of being left out, unable to participate in worship or feasts, 12 years of being rejected and unacceptable, 12 years of feeling like a nobody. She saw Jesus as the only answer she might ever have to solve her problem.

Think what Jesus did for her: Jesus' presence and touch actually healed her. He made her clean—physically, spiritually, and ceremonially. He made her a participant again. He gave her peace. And he made her feel special by not leaving her in the crowd.

No doubt, once Jesus identified her, she must have felt as if she were the only one in the crowd. Jesus didn't let the woman remain as part of the faceless crowd, so he identified her! Jesus actually said, "Be *continually* healed." To the only person he ever called "daughter" he granted continual health.

After this unusual encounter, Jesus overheard that Jairus' daughter was dead. Jesus interjected himself into the situation, encouraging Jairus, the leader of the synagogue, not to be afraid and to have faith. It's interesting that Jesus took his three main men along with him as he went to visit the daughter of Jairus who was presumed to be dead. This is another field trip with his disciples, but this time it's a triple-A miracle that is needed at Jairus' house. The girl is dead and the mourners are well into the mourning process. Jesus goes into her room and raises her from the dead.

These two women serve as great illustrations of hope when you're in the midst of desperate situations, even to the point of death.

Jesus' encounter with the woman who had been bleeding for 12 years is daring, because in her state of health she was unclean. Then note that while Jesus is busy healing a woman who has been unclean for 12 years, Jairus' 12-year-old daughter has died. Now, Jairus' dead daughter has become unclean through her death.

But no matter, Jesus shows up to touch these two unclean women, bringing one instant healing and bringing the other back to life. When Jesus shows up, most often something wonderful happens!

When Jesus Showed Up in Jericho

A most popular Jesus encounter happened in Jericho. When Jesus showed up in Jericho, he did something most

185

revolutionary. Let's check it out together.

Jesus entered Jericho and was passing through. A man was there by the name of Zacchaeus; he was a chief tax collector and was wealthy. He wanted to see who Jesus was, but because he was short he could not see over the crowd. So he ran ahead and climbed a sycamore-fig tree to see him, since Jesus was coming that way.

When Jesus reached the spot, he looked up and said to him, "Zacchaeus, come down immediately. I must stay at your house today." So he came down at once and welcomed him gladly. All the people saw this and began to mutter, "He has gone to be the guest of a sinner."

Zacchaeus stood up and said to the Lord, "Look, Lord! Here and now I give half of my possessions to the poor, and if I have cheated anybody out of anything, I will pay back four times the amount."

Jesus said to him, "Today salvation has come to this house, because this man, too, is a son of Abraham. For the Son of Man came to seek and to save what was lost" (Luke 19).

For many, the encounter with Zaccheus is so familiar and that is the problem. It's so familiar that we continually miss the point Jesus was making. I know I did. Let me explain.

Don't miss the context here. Jericho was the main route to take from the Galilee to Jerusalem. Jesus has made his way through the city of Jericho from the Galilee area to Jerusalem multiple times. This was Jesus' last trip through Jericho to Jerusalem. I can imagine that as Jesus' popularity continued to increase that the religious and political leaders of a city like Jericho would expect to welcome him into their city and host him there.

Jesus enters the city, and the city elders, particularly the religious ones, are there to give him their special welcome. Most likely they had plans to socialize with Jesus over a meal. They were the spiritual ones—the righteous—

of the city of Jericho.

As they greeted Jesus and walked with him through the city, he changed their plans, offended them and threatened their super-spiritual position among the people. Jesus essentially turned down their social entrées and picked out one of the lesser ones—Zaccheus. Zaccheus was not viewed among the social elite within Jericho. He wasn't among the religiously accepted, an alien of sorts. He was the representation of the sinner within the city—the hated tax collector, maybe even was the manager of all of the tax collection in the city.

When Jesus saw him up in the sycamore tree, he noticed him. It's very possible that Jesus knew Zaccheus. Jesus possibly addressed him, "Zack, come on down. Let's hang out together today—at your house!"

Note the people who heard this were shocked and not happy! They began to mutter and grumble over this invitation.

I've always believed that when Zaccheus came down from his perch in the tree and met with Jesus, he confessed his cheating and stealing to Jesus and Jesus offered him salvation. But this is not what happened! Check it out!

Zaccheus didn't have a meeting with Jesus, nor did he confess his cheating and stealing to Jesus. Look at it closely. Zaccheus just landed on his feet at the base of the tree and made his famous statement to Jesus. They had not had any time to talk or discuss his life.

As you take a closer look at what Zaccheus actually said, it changes everything. But Zacchaeus stood up and said to the Lord, "Look, Lord! Here and now I give half of my possessions to the poor, and if I have cheated anybody out of anything, I will pay back four times the amount."

The verbiage is in the present active tense. He is not saying, "Now that I have met you, Jesus, I will give half of what I make to the poor." But, he is a saying, "Jesus, I am presently giving half of what I own to the poor and if anyone believes I have cheated them in any way, I am re-paying them four times the amount." This showed Zac-cheus had confidence he wasn't cheating anyone and was already a charitable man to the poor.

Jesus said to him, "Today salvation has come to this house, because this man, too, is a son of Abraham." I think Jesus set up this divine appointment with Zaccheus to make a point. Zaccheus, the man who doesn't enjoy re-ligious and super-spiritual status, is far more honest and spiritual than those who hold those positions in the city of Jericho. Therefore, this "sinner" possesses salvation and a right standing before God.

Jesus knew Zaccheus, all right. He knew him well. He knew his heart. The point of this encounter is to clarify who is right before God and who is not. And Jesus loved every moment of it!

When Jesus Showed Up in the Book of Acts

The active presence of Jesus is not limited to the 33 years of his life he spent from his birth in Bethlehem to his death and resurrection in Jerusalem. In the Book of Acts Jesus continued to show up among his followers. This is why I like to call the Book of Acts the "Acts of Jesus" and not the "Acts of the Apostles."

Jesus showed up and the result was his followers sharing Jesus' message of the Kingdom to the world (Acts 1). It was important that his followers knew Jesus person-ally, so he spent an additional 40 days with them with lots of personal interaction.

It was important that his followers had a strategy on how to take Jesus' message of the Kingdom throughout the world, so Jesus urged them to wait for his Spirit to come upon them to give them the power to spread this revolu-tionary message to the world.

Jesus showed up through Peter to communicate his message to many nations (Acts 2). Jesus showed up through Peter and John to empower the healing of a lame man (Acts 3). Jesus showed up to empower several articulate moments through his followers (Acts 4, 5, and 7). Jesus showed up to apprehend Paul to bear his name everywhere—to the house of Israel, to the non-Jewish nations of the world, and to their kings (Acts 9). Jesus showed up to demonstrate to Peter that his message must not be contained within a Jewish box, but is for everyone everywhere (Acts 10).

Acts 29—Today!

Several of us who are walking together have found reading the Acts of Jesus one chapter per day can be an amazing experience. We have read it through for several months at a time and it increases our own awareness of when and where Jesus is showing up in our lives today. There are 28 chapters in the Acts of Jesus. We start on the first day of the month reading chapter 1 and a chapter a day according to the monthly calendar through the 28th day of the month. If you want to be more aware of Jesus sightings in your life, pick a month and begin reading through the Acts of Jesus.

It's important to note that Jesus' activity doesn't stop at the end of the 28th chapter. Jesus continues to act each and every day—24 hours a day, 365 days a year. Therefore, we have found it most helpful to move into the rest of our lives with Jesus. We call it Acts 29! Acts 29 is living out your relationship with Jesus today, because Jesus continues to act in and through all followers who have ears to hear and eyes to see.

So today, the Acts of Jesus become most evident as one pays attention to the three essentials in following the revolutionary Jesus.

- The pre-eminence of Jesus, making him first in your life.

- The presence of the Kingdom, living it as your lifestyle.

- The power of the few, following Jesus with a few like-minded traveling companions.

"When and where Jesus shows up" is not just a cliché or hope or mystical experience. It's a reality and we have been experiencing this reality for several years. The Jesus movement was launched when Jesus showed up among his followers and that transformational movement is still on today!

Part V

simply following Jesus plus

nothing

CHAPTER 13

What Is the Jesus Manifesto?

We turn the corner now to a more practical application of following Jesus. Up to this point, we have discussed what it means to miss the point of Jesus by burying him under innumerable add-ons and leaving him out of our lives, that he is the pre-eminent one of all who have ever lived, that he came to introduce humankind to the Kingdom of God, and that the primary way to live out the Kingdom principles is to embrace and live out the Jesus lifestyle in the context of a few.

So, these final chapters are designed to help you embrace Jesus as a lifestyle.

- "What Is the Jesus Manifesto?" discusses the core of Jesus' teachings.

- "What Does It Mean to Be a Follower of Jesus?" demonstrates how you follow Jesus.

- "What Are the Three Vital Habits in Following Jesus?" safeguards how you continue to follow Jesus.

- "What Does It Look Like to Show Off Jesus?" discloses the five most effective ways to communicate Jesus.

- "What Is Your End Game?" exposes your hidden, however well-intentioned, agendas.

Through these final chapters I want to invite you to become a follower of Jesus. I promise there will be no proselytizing, no converting, no rejecting your cultural background, no changing of your religious affiliation, only a personal invitation to follow Jesus.

It seems appropriate to begin this section with Jesus' first seminar—the most amazing seminar he ever taught! I have always referred to it as "The Jesus Manifesto." Years ago I was so compelled to study only this teaching of Jesus that I concentrated all of my reading and study on it for six months. I purposed to know nothing but this powerful teaching as thoroughly as I could. That intense exercise proved to be the best foundational experience for me and launched me into a search to know Jesus and his teachings better.

If you want to understand the essence of Jesus and his teachings, immerse yourself into these three chapters in Matthew (5-7). Memorize this section! Meditate on it! Personalize it! Pray for Jesus to change your heart through these revolutionary words! It's only a little over 2500 words long. You'll learn more in these words of Jesus than you'll ever be able to apply! If you dare to embrace these teachings for yourself, Jesus will turn your world and thinking inside out and upside down. If you humbly ingest these thoughts, you will discover personal satisfaction.

At the time of this seminar, Jesus is the new rabbi (teacher) in town. He has already chosen a few men to follow him closely—to be taught in his ways. Being a new teacher, the question automatically arises: "Jesus, how does your teaching differ from what we've been taught?" This question is relevant for every one of us today, no matter your cultural or religious background. How do the teachings of Jesus differ from what we've been taught so far?

Jesus sets out to answer this underlying question for the people then and for us now. This is the most dynamic and revolutionary section of Jesus' teachings. Jesus' teachings are so outside the box that many theologians and ministers have relegated "The Jesus Manifesto" to a later time in the future Kingdom and not applicable for life today. But this is precisely the point of what Jesus is saying. These are Kingdom teachings and principles—life on a higher plane. Jesus said the Kingdom is near, it is within reach and is among us.

The theme of Jesus' message seems to be all about true righteousness. Now don't let that term throw you. Righteousness is merely to be in right standing before God. To be righteous is to live your life consistently with God's standard. The religious of Jesus' day and of our present day all have a list of do's and don'ts to attain a right standing before God. Jesus' plan counters all other plans for being right before God. The Jesus Manifesto is worthy of a full book, but for the purposes of this book I want to briefly highlight Jesus' teachings on the best way to live in the Kingdom. As I draw out several of Jesus' radical teachings, you will quickly notice that the Jesus lifestyle moves to the beat of a different drummer. The drummer is Jesus, himself!

A Portrait of Living the Kingdom Life (Matthew 5)

Jesus presents eight teachings of what a happy, blessed Kingdom lifestyle looks like. The first four are all about our personal relationship with God on the inside. The second four extend the first four out into our relationships with others. It is truly a great pattern for first walking with Jesus and then walking with others, or as Jesus put it, "Love God and love your neighbor as yourself." Remember, these are all comparing Jesus' teachings with what we've been taught.

Jesus carefully describes each of these eight dimensions with very few words. Each one begins with "happy" or "blessed are you," when you are this way or that. "You'll do well to be this way" is his point in every one or, to put it another way, "the Kingdom citizen looks like this."

Jesus is speaking to a large group of people who have

been taught by some haughty authority figures who have spent their lives outlining what it means to be righteous before God and that system is really a performance system of attempting some level of perfection. Let's look at each of these dimensions, commonly referred to as "The Beatitudes."

(1) "Blessed are the poor in spirit, for theirs is the kingdom of heaven."

Jesus begins at the opposite end of the spectrum. He starts out turning upside down what most had been taught. Kingdom righteousness begins when you understand your spiritual poverty, another way of saying, your total need for God.

To be poor in spirit means to have a right evaluation of yourself, of God, and of others. All of life begins at this point. Possessing a right evaluation of yourself before self, God, and others is true humility—the exact opposite of the blindness of pride. Pride is one of the seven deadly sins; it's universal among humans and it's devastating! Pride always seeks to be exalted, to be first, and to be praised.

(2) "Blessed are those who mourn, for they will be comforted."

Now wait a minute! Jesus begins with our spiritual bankruptcy and now talks about mourning? *Blessed* are those who mourn? Are you kidding? How can mourning be a blessed experience or one that makes you happy? As you can see, every one of these snapshots goes against what you might normally expect. Jesus and his Kingdom always move to the beat of a different drummer.

Mourning is a sensitivity to that which keeps you from being and doing all that you were created to be and to do. This snapshot builds right on top of the first—affirming your poverty. Once you have a right evaluation of yourself, of God, and of others, it is natural to be more sensitive to anything that might pull you down or pull you away from doing what's right. It's really mourning over that which keeps you from Jesus and his Kingdom.

> *(3)* "Blessed are the meek, for they will inherit the earth."

This third teaching builds on the first two—poor in spirit and mourning. Meekness is not weakness. It's a quiet, controlled, inner strength—a mark of God on your life. Once you see clearly who you really are (poor in spirit), you are ready for growth. Then, as you mourn over that which keeps you from growing, you actually graduate through this pile of problems. Now, you can't remain under the pile of mourning; you gain inner strength as you emerge from the pile. If you remain there in your mourning, you will tend to be content to wallow in your weaknesses, singing "Woe is me . . . " Many people seem to enjoy suffering like this. We can easily find a new friend in depression or loss or a sickness. They find that people seem to care more for them when they're wallowing in a problem, so they take that problem on as their identity—sort of a badge of courage. Don't wallow in your sorrows. Recognize them. See them for what they are. Mourn them. And grow through them!

> *(4)* "Blessed are those who hunger and thirst for righteousness, for they will be filled."

The first three teachings speak of what we all lack. This fourth teaching fills in all of the lacking areas with being satisfied or filled. Note the strong terms here—hunger and thirst, not simply desiring something or making it a high priority. This is desperation—just like our need for food and water, we have the same need for our souls. The kind of desperation that has a full understanding of your need for God, a desperate kind of mourning and an attitude of meekness. At this point of desperation you are ready for hungering and thirsting for righteousness—for anything that is right and pure and good.

Hungering and thirsting for righteousness is a refocusing of your heart, developing a passion for filling up the hole in your soul. Everybody is passionately seeking inner satisfaction. This fourth teaching or attitude is a kind of hungering and thirsting for what you want in your innermost being.

Remember, "righteousness" is right living. It's walking consistently with God's standard. Jesus was the Righteous One who walked most consistently with God's standard. In a very real sense, there is no other standard. God's standard for living life is the only one you were created to follow. All other standards are not standards at all, but scattered attempts to live life without God. Many of these attempts are couched in what we know as *religion*—religious systems of do's and don'ts to attain some level of approval by God—to reach some heavenly state and to avoid going to hell. Unfortunately, man's best attempts are like going to heaven on a six-foot ladder. The problem with this method is that the ladder can only go up six feet.

Do you want to find satisfaction in your soul? Then hunger and thirst after Jesus and his Kingdom everyday! It's the only possible way to this kind of serenity and satisfaction. This is what I mean by refocusing your heart! It's only when sensing your emptiness revealed within the first three snapshots that you have access to spiritual fullness. These are the quiet cravings—the hungering and thirsting—for spiritual things, for the inner satisfaction of your soul! Refocus your heart on hungering and thirsting.

The first four teachings or beatitudes are about your relationship before God. They are quite personal—poor in spirit, mourning, meekness, hungering and thirsting for righteousness. The second four are internal qualities also before God, yet regarding your relationship with others.

(5) "Blessed are the merciful, for they will receive mercy."

To be merciful is to reach out with compassion. This means to identify with other people's needs in a compassionate way. Initiate a positive effect toward the people in the world around you.

There is no way you will be able to reach out with compassion or be merciful without the dimension of being poor in spirit. Poor in spirit is a pre-requisite for being merciful to others. In other words, if you want to check out how you can reach out with compassion more effectively, start with reaffirming your poverty. Start with checking whether or not you are poor in spirit. This makes so much sense when you think about it. It's very difficult to show compassion to another person, when you are filled with pride and haughtiness. On the other hand, when you are a person who has a right evaluation of yourself, God, and others, you are freed up to be able to show genuine compassion to others. When you have received grace from God, it's much easier to give out mercy.

(6) "Blessed are the pure in heart, for they will see God."

In the same way, being merciful emerges out your spiritual poverty, being pure in heart springs out of your mourning. On the surface being "pure in heart" doesn't appear to have much to do with others. However, being pure in heart is about being loyal, honest, and trustworthy as a friend. In Proverbs it says "the king's friend is pure in heart." Pure in heart is one who can be counted on at all times—a safe person to have on your team.

Being a loyal friend and enjoying loyal friends is the community context for the vibrant Jesus movement. Note that safe friends are those who mourn—those who have sensitivity to that which keeps them from following after Jesus. When you are comforted, you are freed up to comfort and support others.

Everyone is in desperate need of the dynamic of friendship. Without friendship you wither, and eventually parts of you that were once vibrant and full of life begin to die.

(7) "Blessed are the peacemakers, for they will be
called sons of God."

To be a peacemaker requires that you make peace where there is no peace. Be aware of trouble, distress, brokenness, and of those who are living in pieces. You don't have to look too far. Listen to those around you. There is a great void—a great need to be understood in our world or in our circle of friends. In fact, you probably won't even have to search for it, just listen and be aware. This teaching carries with it the dynamic message of Jesus—peace where there is no peace.

Being a peacemaker emerges out of the teaching on meekness. Remember that meekness is a quiet, controlled, inner strength. You don't have a chance to be a peacemaker without these qualities. Without the attitude of meekness you have the tendency to be reactive rather than proactive, which is what restoring peace requires. Meekness is the inner quality that allows you to be a peacemaker.

I like the simple prayer that says: "Dear Lord, as in the world I toil and through this world I flit, I pray make me a drop of oil and not a piece of grit!" The lifestyle of Jesus for his Kingdom followers is to be a peacemaker.

(8) "Blessed are those who have been persecuted
for the sake of righteousness, for theirs is the
kingdom of heaven. Blessed are you when

people insult you and persecute you, and falsely
say all kinds of evil against you because of Me.

Rejoice and be glad, for your reward in heaven
is great; for in the same way they persecuted the
prophets who were before you."

To rejoice in persecution is to develop the big picture
on all troubles—especially the trouble that others bring.
Life is full of stress and distress. Many of life's stresses are
circumstantial. Some are spiritual. Some are physical. Some
are emotional.

Note the reason for persecution here. It's that same
word we saw earlier—righteousness. As you hunger and
thirst for righteousness—being like Jesus (allowing him to
live his life through you)—some people will become un-
comfortable and you may begin to see them pick away at
you.

Also note the kinds of persecution mentioned: it's
insults, falsely saying all kinds of evil against you because
of the Jesus and the Kingdom lifestyle you are embracing.
Notice who is doing the persecuting in the New Testament
against the early followers of Jesus, and you will quickly
find that this kind of persecution comes from other religious people who are jealous and threatened.

Jesus says that when you are persecuted or criticized
in this way, your best response is to rejoice and be glad.
This could be translated as rejoice and celebrate! What is
most encouraging is that they have noticed something different about you. You are growing up. You are beginning
to find a personal satisfaction that sets you apart. Your response must be to redouble your efforts in refocusing your
heart even more. You'll need it to truly rejoice in the midst
of this kind of persecution. Keep on hungering and thirsting for that inner, spiritual satisfaction for your soul. Then
rejoice in persecution. It is a cause for celebration because

your inner transformation has become outwardly visible.

All eight teachings are wrapped up in a package—all describing what a citizen of the Kingdom looks like. What a picture it is! Take on these attitudes for yourself. Meditate on them and discover the great depth within them. They offer you the ingredients that will produce the most valuable and powerful emotional riches you could ever experience. I have spent most of my life meditating and referring back to these eight dynamic teachings. Make them yours. Go back to them often. Maybe even memorize them and ask God to emblazon them on your soul.

The Precepts of Kingdom Living (Matthew 5)

Jesus continues his revolutionary teaching by comparing his teachings to Six Laws from the Mosaic Law in Matthew 5. Two of the most radical have to do with anger and lust. Jesus says, "You have heard it said that you should not commit murder, but I say to you that if you have anger and hate, you have already committed murder in your heart."

Then Jesus says, "You have heard it said that you are not to commit adultery, but I say that if you have lusted after a woman, you have already committed adultery in your heart." Each of these gives a good picture of Jesus' emphasis upon the heart of the matter rather than outward performance. By doing this, Jesus heightens the seriousness of paying attention to your heart. That's living life the Jesus way in his Kingdom.

The Practices of Kingdom Living (Matthew 6)

Jesus criticizes the practices of the religious community as they show off their "righteousness" for the sake of showing themselves as more spiritual than all others. Jesus uses three practices in Matthew 6 to illustrate his point here—

giving, praying, and fasting. Followers of Jesus don't make a spectacle of themselves to be seen by people. These practices are to be directed to God and not before people. So, no public prayer gatherings, no public spectacle of who is giving and how much they have given, and no public spectacle of fasting to seem more holy than others. Jesus is not impressed! This is Jesus' principle of private focus. Some things are only to be acted out between you and God and not for public consumption. Jesus says God will reward followers who practice the principle of private focus. No one has to seek public rewards or attention for these practices.

The Priority of Kingdom Living (Matthew 6)

Also in Matthew 6, Jesus warns against adding other gods to the God of gods, both in your heart and what the eye is focused upon. Once he articulates his principle of single-mindedness, Jesus urges those who embrace the Kingdom lifestyle not to worry, but to count on the God of gods to come through. Therefore, "Seek first God's Kingdom and his righteousness, and you won't be tempted to worry about the material things in life." Jesus teaches that worry can't help you, won't change anything, and is counterproductive.

The Perseverance of Kingdom Living (Matthew 7)

Eugene Peterson's paraphrase of the Bible, titled, *The Message,* captures Jesus' closing section of his manifesto on Kingdom living in Matthew 7: "Don't look for shortcuts to God. The market is flooded with surefire, easygoing formulas for a successful life that can be practiced in your spare time. Don't fall for that stuff, even though crowds of people do. The way to life—to God!—is vigorous and requires total attention.

"Be wary of false preachers who smile a lot, dripping

with practiced sincerity. Chances are they are out to rip you off some way or other. Don't be impressed with charisma; look for character. Who preachers are is the main thing, not what they say. A genuine leader will never exploit your emotions or your pocketbook. These diseased trees with their bad apples are going to be chopped down and burned.

"Knowing the correct password—saying 'Master, Master,' for instance—isn't going to get you anywhere with me. What is required is serious obedience—doing what my Father wills. I can see it now—at the Final Judgment thousands strutting up to me and saying, 'Master, we preached the Message, we bashed the demons, our God-sponsored projects had everyone talking.' And do you know what I am going to say? 'You missed the boat. All you did was use me to make yourselves important. You don't impress me one bit. You're out of here.'

"These words I speak to you are not incidental additions to your life, homeowner improvements to your standard of living. They are foundational words, words to build a life on. If you work these words into your life, you are like a smart carpenter who built his house on solid rock. Rain poured down, the river flooded, a tornado hit—but nothing moved that house. It was fixed to the rock.

"But if you just use my words in Bible studies and don't work them into your life, you are like a stupid carpenter who built his house on the sandy beach. When a storm rolled in and the waves came up, it collapsed like a house of cards."

When Jesus concluded his address, the crowd burst into applause. They had never heard teaching like this. It was apparent that he was living everything he was saying— quite a contrast to their religious teachers! This was the best teaching they had ever heard.

We have only had an overview of the Jesus Manifesto in this chapter. As you can see, Jesus stands above the religious leadership of his day *and* today. His teachings are so powerful and practical, yet so counter-intuitive. There's nothing common about his teachings. And there's nothing easy about them, either. Yet every time I hear Jesus' words, they resonate with my heart. I suspect they do in yours, as well.

All this brings us to a most personal question:

How can *I* follow this Jesus?

CHAPTER 14

What Does It Mean to Be a Follower of Jesus?

After Jesus described what it means to be a happy, blessed, and fulfilled follower, he uses two dynamic roles to position his followers in this world—salt and light. "You are the salt of the earth. But if the salt loses its saltiness, how can it be made salty again? It is no longer good for anything, except to be thrown out and trampled underfoot" (Matthew 5).

Jesus says, "You *are* the salt of the earth!" It's not that you might be or you could be, but you *are*. Salt was used as a preservative to counteract the decay in meat. In order for salt to be effective it must be out of the saltshaker and applied to the meat.

Salt is like the invisible presence of God. It must be sensed. You're the salt in the world around you—the invisible presence of God among those you touch. Just by your presence there is to be a preserving of purity, honesty, and fairness.

A saltless disciple is good for nothing except to be thrown out and trampled under foot. Jesus uses the term tasteless. The original Greek word is *moraino*, which means to be foolish—to play the fool, insipid, dull, flat, or deficient.

In rabbinic literature, salt is associated with wisdom—a foolish disciple has no impact on his world. Also, salt adds flavor to things. Jesus is to life what salt is to food. Jesus and the Kingdom lend flavor to life to be a difference-maker. The world is changed by flavoring it with your salt-like presence.

It was Saint Francis of Assisi who said, "preach the gospel at all times, and when necessary use words." This is precisely what it means to be salt.

"You are the light of the world. A city on a hill cannot be hidden. Neither do people light a lamp and put it under a bowl. Instead they put it on its stand, and it gives light to everyone in the house. In the same way, let your light shine before others, that they may see your good deeds and glorify your Father in heaven" (Matthew 5).

Note again Jesus says, "You *are* the light of the world!" Salt has a powerful, invisible nature to it; light is more like the visible presence of God. Salt must be sensed—light must be seen! Light counteracts darkness.

The visible presence of God consists of the essence of salt and the radiance of light. It must be attractive and authentic! The core of this light can be found in loving your neighbor as yourself. We are beyond the point where mere talk—no matter how sound—can make an impression. Demonstration is required. We must live what we talk, even in places where we cannot talk what we live. The test is reality—authenticity—the genuine!

Whereas salt was a warning against being good for nothing, light is used to show us how to be good for something. It is the outer or doing side of these two images used by Jesus. You *are* the salt of the earth and the light of the world; you *are* the invisible and visible presence of God on planet earth. Don't become tasteless salt. Don't cover up your light. Allow Jesus to be sensed in you and seen in you.

Jesus made it clear what he expected his early followers to do. Initially, Jesus expressed his most revolutionary call: *Follow me!* At the very end of Matthew's Gospel, Jesus says: "All authority in heaven and on earth has been given to me. Therefore, make disciples of all nations, by going, by baptizing, and teaching them to obey everything I have commanded you. And surely I am with you always, to the very end of the age" (Matthew 28).

Whatever Jesus is saying here, it is important that you see what was on Jesus' heart in these last words for his followers. Jesus presents one command here; it's not an option. Jesus makes it clear that he wants his followers *to make disciples of all nations.*

This is not to make Christians of all nations or Westerners of all nations or Church members of all nations. This command is about making disciples of all nations.

The term "disciple" is only used in the five Gospels (including Acts); it cannot be found in the rest of the New Testament. A disciple is literally a learner—one who listens and follows a teacher and his teachings. Jesus commands his disciples to go make disciples of all nations. As described earlier, "nations" is best understood as cultures. We're realizing that no matter what culture is introduced to Jesus, the response is amazingly positive and transformational. And just as Jesus gave this command to his first disciples, it's clear that Jesus wants all of his disciples everywhere to continue to multiply more disciples. This has nothing to do with converting or proselytizing anyone, but encouraging people in the cultures of the world to become followers of Jesus.

To me, a disciple is simply a follower of Jesus—one who hears Jesus' teachings and seeks to practice them. We are doing our best to be faithful disciples of Jesus and to introduce him into the many cultures of our world. We see ourselves as followers of Jesus, not Christians or believers or church members. We say it this way among our friends: "We're trying to do the most difficult thing we have ever done in our lives. We're trying to follow the teachings and principles of Jesus." This is discipleship—to know Jesus and to make him known.

A disciple—a learner and follower of Jesus—must make it his or her single-minded focus to be like Jesus as best he can. Simply put, see and hear what Jesus does and do it!

Three Requirements of a Follower

Although there are many and varied lists of what it means to be a Jesus follower, it seems counter-productive to choose a series of characteristics to follow. Here's the problem. Once you have a list, there is a tendency to follow the list and not Jesus.

As we make our way through some thoughts on what it means to be a disciple of Jesus, it's important to take him at his word on the subject before quoting anyone else. I invite you to check out these discipleship requirements for yourself.

At one point, Jesus turned to the many who were following him and challenged them to be his true disciples. He presented three very tough requirements in order to be a disciple—a genuine follower of Jesus. They are still tough, but after attempting to live them out, the benefits far outweigh not doing so.

Let's join the crowds of people who were following alongside Jesus for a variety of reasons. Luke writes, "Now as Jesus proceeded on his journey, great crowds accompanied him and he turned and spoke to them, 'If anyone comes to me without setting aside his relationship with his father and mother and wife and children and brothers and sisters, and even his own life, he cannot be a disciple of mine" (Luke 14).

In the statement above, Jesus declares the first of three prerequisites to be one of his disciples—*the requirement of priority*. There are many reasons people might follow Jesus, but if you want to in fact be a disciple of Jesus, it is necessary to make Jesus number one above all others. He makes it tougher than just saying that he wants to be your best friend after your family members. He requires that you set aside your family members—father, mother, wife, children, brothers, and sisters—to reduce in importance your family members in comparison with your relationship with Jesus. He is to be your #1 priority. You go to him first. He makes it even more personal, when he says to set aside "even your own life."

Jesus wants all who desire to be his disciple to place him above all of their own self-interests. This is the area where we create many of our own little gods that we have come to worship and put ahead of or equal to Jesus. You cannot be full of yourself and be acting as a disciple—a follower of Jesus—at the same time. There is not enough room in your heart for that balancing act.

Jesus is often quoted as saying that he requires you to hate your family and to hate yourself. Jesus spoke in Aramaic and in that language the wording is clearly not "hate," but to "set aside" all others to make Jesus your highest priority.

Then, note that Jesus doesn't equivocate at all here. He says unless you put him as the highest priority in your life—the highest position of authority, "you cannot be my disciple." It's not that you cannot be a good disciple or one of the better disciples or a better than average disciple; it's that you cannot be a disciple of his at all. There is no wiggle room here. Jesus sets the bar very high, even unreachable for many of us at times. Yet what I want in my heart of hearts is to make him my highest priority. Jesus sets up this requirement as a dynamic end game for us to place our single-minded focus upon.

Will you allow me to get personal with you again? So, *do* you want to be a disciple of Jesus? Then, make him your number one, above all others. Make him the person you go to, the one you consult first, and the one you imitate most. The way I see this done is that Jesus wants you to walk with him so closely that you don't start your day, enter into a meeting, begin a conversation, respond to a crisis, react to an enemy, or end your day without talking with him first.

This is what it means to make him your priority! Will you take this challenge from Jesus and make him your priority? It doesn't mean to ignore anyone, because we show our love for Jesus in the act of loving others. And you can be sure this is not a call to perfection, but a channeling of your heart's focus.

Jesus declares the second prerequisite to be one of his disciples—*the requirement of perseverance.* The requirement of perseverance is to make Jesus your priority—no matter what happens to you! Your relationship with Jesus is your highest priority and you will not be deterred from following him and shaping your life after him by anything. You will hang in there no matter what—no matter the troubles you face or the stress-filled identification that arises because of your association with Jesus.

Here's how Jesus states this requirement: "The man who will not carry his cross and follow in my footsteps cannot be my disciple" (Luke 14). Jesus' disciple must carry the cross just as Jesus did—following in the footsteps of Jesus. If you are unwilling to do this, then you cannot be his disciple.

So, what does Jesus mean by "carry your cross"? The cross of Jesus was the greatest expression of sacrificial love ever. Here is God's Messiah—the most powerful person ever born—and his ultimate act was a demonstration of love, not power. The Roman Empire's symbol was the cross—an emblem of domination and power, because of their method of discipline—crucifixion. Jesus literally turned the cross upside down and inside out to turn this symbol of cruelty and power into the ultimate symbol of sacrificial love.

Jesus' plan was to demonstrate the love of God to the world by allowing himself to die on that Roman cross— transforming the terrifying symbol of the cross into a symbol of hope, peace, and grace. Now that's the greatest example of sacrificial love ever and triggered the Jesus movement that has transformed more lives and cultures than any other movement in all history.

So, what does it mean for you to carry your cross? I think it has to do with identifying your mission in life so much with Jesus that you actually incarnate him—or flesh him out. Carrying your cross is to be a sacrificial lover—to be Jesus in all you say and do. The experience of the cross was one of shame and degradation. Carrying Jesus' cross requires a certain perseverance to follow Jesus, even when faced with that same kind of shame and degradation.

Normally, when Jesus talks about the cross and discipleship, he uses the word to "take up" the cross. Luke uses a different word here. He uses the word that means to carry or bear the cross as opposed to taking up or picking up your cross. The term Luke uses is not something you carry, but something that is attached to you. It's the same term Luke uses when he talks about Paul's mission to bear the name of Jesus to the gentiles, their kings and to the house of Israel. The root word is to walk with or carry the name of Jesus—to be so identified with Jesus' name that he is not only Paul's partner but his identity (Acts 9).

Paul didn't have to pick up the cross; he was already attached to Jesus. When you carry the cross, you are actually so identified with Jesus that you are to be Jesus to the world around you. It's to be proactive with the love of Jesus rather than reactive against whatever or whoever assaults you.

There is a cost in carrying your cross. Following Jesus as your highest priority and fleshing him out in your life will stir up lots of controversy. When you take the path of Jesus versus the normal ways of religious living, you may suffer some negative consequences. Being like Jesus, choosing the sacrificial love approach will most certainly separate you from most religious people, because you are like Jesus, a contrarian, going against the religious grain.

A sad thing happened as the church of Jesus became

organized, the cross took on that same idea of domination and power within the church itself. The organized Church of Christendom took on the power of being the only channel for salvation and communication with God. From the Roman Empire to Jesus to organized Christianity, the symbol of the cross went full circle. To carry the cross of Jesus in his footsteps is to resist this domination and power motif and to reverse the momentum back to the sacrificial love of Jesus. You may find great resistance as you take this on as a lifestyle.

Another consequence of carrying your cross is that you must endure everything that is thrown at you—trials, troubles, stresses, injustices, and all kinds of things that will require you to give of yourself in a sacrificial way. When you think you can't take it any longer, you still hang on. It's the requirement of perseverance—hanging in there with Jesus no matter what!

As we have learned to follow Jesus more closely, we are amazed at what opportunities and oppositions come our way. More and more is asked of us as we walk this walk. Again, this is why I say, "This is the toughest thing I've ever tried to do—to follow the teachings and principles of Jesus."

Jesus declares the third prerequisite to be one of his disciples—*the requirement of how you possess your possessions.* It's all a matter of where you place your dependence.

This final requirement Jesus presents may be the toughest of all. Before he actually presents it, Jesus offers two illustrations that strongly urge you to count the cost of what it means to follow Jesus. The first has to do with the building of a tower: "If any of you wanted to build a tower, wouldn't he first sit down and work out the cost of it to see if he can afford to finish it? Otherwise, when he has laid the foundation and found himself unable to complete the building, everyone who sees it will begin to jeer at him, saying, 'This is the man who started to build a tower but couldn't finish it'" (Luke 14).

Then, Jesus illustrates counting the cost with a king going off to war against another king: "Or, suppose there is a king who is going to war with another king, doesn't he sit down first and consider whether he can engage the twenty thousand of the other king with his own ten thousand? And if he decides he can't, then while the other king is still a long way off, he sends messengers to him to ask for conditions of peace" (Luke 14).

Then Jesus reveals his third requirement: "So it is with you; only the man who says goodbye to all his possessions can be my disciple" (Luke 14). Or, to put it another way: "In the same way, those of you who do not give up everything you have cannot be my disciples." Naturally, the wording "give up everything" is the operative phrase here. What does it mean to give up everything? I like the first translation best: "say goodbye to all of your possessions." That says it well! The Greek word here means to "take leave" or "renounce" your possessions. We briefly referred to this in one of the myths about Jesus. Jesus is not saying that you are to give over all your possessions, but to give them up— to renounce ownership of all you have. You really *don't* own what you have. You are a manager or steward of what God has allowed you to collect. Jesus wants you to realize this and be willing to give up your personal ownership of all you have for Jesus and the Kingdom. Jesus wants you to hold on to your stuff, but hold it loosely and be ready to share generously as it is needed. It's really giving up your dependence on it and depending on Jesus instead.

It's even more than this. You are not just to give up everything you have, but all you are as well—your very existence! This is inherent in the word used for possessions. He owns it all—you and all of your stuff! It's learning to wear the cloak of materialism loosely and to live your life as one who is owned and directed by Jesus. So, make Jesus your highest priority over all relationships, make him your priority no matter what and renounce the ownership of all you are and have. These are the requirements of being a disciple of Jesus.

The spirit of these discipleship requirements is all about surrender—abandoning all competing relationships and securities for Jesus and the Kingdom. There are many examples of surrender, and it isn't the same for all. Some of Jesus' first disciples, Peter, James, and John, left their fishing business to follow Jesus full-time. Levi also left his position at the local tax collections office. Zacchaeus did not leave his vocation, but he did give half his fortune to the poor. There is the rich young ruler who was unwilling to renounce his wealth and follow Jesus. He walked away with great sadness. Paul, from the book of Acts, didn't leave his profession of making tents; he was able to take his profession with him wherever he went.

Diana and I are devoting ourselves to practicing these three very tough requirements of Jesus. What's interesting is that the more closely you follow alongside Jesus the easier it is to live as a disciple. Living like this has been a graduate school experience of how to walk with Jesus, walk with others, and to wait on Jesus to lead out with orders and opportunities.

CHAPTER 15

What Are the Three Vital Habits in Following Jesus?

It's not my intention to offer you list after list of things you *must do* in order to follow Jesus. Most of my life teaching and preaching I had three steps to do this or five steps to do that. If you had done this on a weekly basis as I had done it for over 25 years, the pile would be quite a list of things to do. Where can anyone find the time to apply these lists, even if they were the truth? That approach said, "Follow Jesus Tim's way." Not any more!

Since doing my best to stubbornly follow Jesus, I've come to a few conclusions:

#1—I have no agenda. This is extremely freeing for all, not just for me but for everyone I encounter.

#2—I have no answers. I used to have all of the answers, but now I realize I don't know nearly as much as I thought I did.

#3—Jesus is the only answer I know. I have come to realize he has all of the answers, so I refer most people to him.

#4—Jesus works without an agenda as he is lifted up.

#5—Jesus is the best news for any bad news that presents itself. Jesus, simply Jesus.

Consequently, the purpose of this book is to share with you only two things: What Jesus said and did, along with my personal experience, strength, and hope in following Jesus with a few traveling companions.

In this chapter I want to share with you three vital habits we practice in following Jesus. These habits not only summarize what we have learned in following Jesus; they will give you several new handles on how to follow Jesus in your world.

Let me illustrate this approach in this way. Three pastors from a local mega-church asked me to meet with them. I agreed, and they posed a fascinating question. They asked, "How can we, as pastors, follow Jesus?" This perceptive question came as quite a shock to me! I loved it!

My response was immediate. I said, "I have absolutely no idea how you can follow Jesus as pastors, but I am willing to walk through this question with you. I have no doubt that you can figure it out as we walk together." We did, and they did!

As a simple and stubborn follower of Jesus I have found it's vital to embrace three basic habits for yourself. It's been said that to develop a habit, you must do something for three weeks. It's also been said, if you practice your habit everyday for 6 weeks, you'll own it for yourself. In other words . . . watch your thoughts; they become words. Watch your words; they become actions. Watch your actions; they become habits. Watch your habits; they become character. Watch your character; it becomes your destiny.

I want to encourage you to practice these simple habits as you do your best to be a follower of Jesus:

Habit #1—Walking with Jesus

Walking with Jesus means you are devoted to Jesus.
- *Devoted to imitate Jesus*—to walk, talk, love, and think like Jesus. The question to check this is "What Did Jesus Do?" (WDJD?) Follow him.

- *Devoted to consult with Jesus* regarding your personal, family, and professional decisions. The question to check this is "What Would Jesus Do?" (WWJD?) This is slightly different from "WDJD?" This is following what Jesus would do in a given situation.

- *Devoted to converse with Jesus* throughout your day. Prayer is simply a conversation within your relationship with Jesus. The question to check this is "What Is Jesus Saying?" (WIJS?)

- *Devoted to community the way Jesus was*—disciplining yourself to do life with a few others. The question to check this is "What Is Jesus Doing?" (WIJD?)

As a friend of mine said, "It's like the announcement that is made on every flight. 'Put your oxygen mask on first and then help those around you.'" Walking with Jesus is just like that. Put on your oxygen mask—your personal relationship with Jesus. That's what comes first—always! Walking with Jesus is being aware of his constant presence in your life. It's being with him, hanging out with him and in a constant dependence on his strength and his lead. Walking with Jesus is learning to count on him in your everyday life. In simple terms, do what he says. No matter what he says to do and say, you just do it. I heard it in a funny way several years ago: "If you pray for a Cadillac and God sends a jackass, ride it." It's signing off as king of your kingdom and making Jesus the King of all kings. This reminds me of the bumper sticker that says: "Want to hear God laugh? Tell him your plans." To walk with Jesus is to be willing to let him direct your life.

Habit #2—Walking with Others

As always, Jesus is our example of this habit. When he began his ministry, he chose three to come alongside him—to be with him. He continued to spend most of his time with these three. This small group expanded to 12, then the 72, and then the 120. In fact, at one point there are up to 500 who were fairly close disciples of Jesus. I'm sure most everyone who followed Jesus felt close to him, yet he walked mostly with a few.

Jesus also sent his early disciples out in pairs, not alone, and then the early disciples continued to follow Jesus' example. They continued to model this by spending time together, studying the teachings of Jesus, eating, praying, and fellowshipping with one another.

Walking with others is a commitment to be in community with a few, in conversation with Jesus with that few and encouraging one another to be like Jesus.

Walking with others provides a level of personal support that we all need. Walking with others provides strength to handle whatever may come in life. There's something about knowing you are not alone that empowers. Without others in your life you are weakened and at your lowest. Encouragement is easily drained, yet within a few trusted friends you will find yourself fueled by the others who are doing life with you. Without others you can easily become distracted, even discouraged.

Diana and I continue to experience this empowerment as we walk with a few. We just don't act on our own any longer. We seek the counsel of our small group and act—travel, teach, and write—with their blessing and support. This family of Jesus followers who are committing to do life with us know they are invited to offer any and all counsel, including, if necessary, confrontation. We now do everything in the strength and affirmation of our dear friends. This is not a one-way street. We feel the same freedom to speak into their lives.

A learning dynamic presents itself within a smaller setting. When walking with others, it's so much easier to experience how others are living the principles of Jesus. When you walk with others your seeing and hearing seem to be better. If you want ears to hear and eyes to see Jesus, operate within a group.

Finally and most importantly, walking with others is a sure place where Jesus will show up. Without others you tend to forget how real and present Jesus is. Walking with others is one of those disciplines of life that produces great results for you and those with whom you are walking.

Living fully requires that you walk with Jesus. When you walk with him, you are the walking solution to people's needs everywhere. And the only way to faithfully walk with Jesus is to walk together. Paul was a master at including others. He must have been a southerner, because he used what I call "the y'all principle" throughout most of his writing. He does this by using the plural form of you. Take a look: "Let the word of Christ richly dwell within you (among y'all), with all wisdom teaching and admonishing one another with psalms and hymns and spiritual songs, singing with thankfulness in your hearts to God" (Colossians 3). Or, "I am again in labor until Christ is formed in you (in y'all)" (Galatians 4). Or, "Christ in you (in y'all), the hope of glory" (Colossians 1).

Paul is commanding believers everywhere to allow Jesus to make his dwelling place (make himself at home) as you come together into the fellowship. The dynamite (power) of the gospel will be present in the midst of a few who are gathered together in Jesus' name. The y'all principle is the fellowship principle and the practice of the presence of the Kingdom.

It is amazing how simple agreements and commitments to one another provide a bonding power among the participants. These covenants may be agreements to pray for certain things for a certain time period, going on a trip together, producing an event, or agreements to go through a study together. This is the fellowship principle! He is calling you into the fellowship of Jesus and his people.

We have found this y'all dynamic of fellowship with a few friends. We meet weekly—studying the teachings of Jesus, eating, praying, and enjoying fellowship together.

This is not a highly homogeneous group of people. In fact, we continually joke about how unlikely it is that we would be together. Our diversity with respect to age, politics, education, careers, backgrounds, and values is enormous, yet our love for Jesus and one another holds us together.

We have walked together through a myriad of family crises, a variety of cancers, death of family members and friends, financial disasters, vocational changes, political elections and the death of one of our group. We walk through life stronger, because we are together, because we love each other and because we are committed to get one another through whatever comes our way. We enjoy practicing the habit of walking with one another.

Habit #3—Waiting on Jesus to Lead Out

It's not only waiting on Jesus to lead out, but waiting on Jesus to lead out with orders and opportunities. Learning this habit and really getting it was the toughest for me. This requires the discipline of trust. And, as if that weren't enough, I've learned you must let go of the results and turn them over to Jesus, too.

As you practice waiting, there is the *action of readying yourself.* Your responsibility is not to be in charge, but to be ready for the King's orders.

As you practice waiting, there is the *action of relating to Jesus and to others*—the first two habits. Your responsibility is to continue these relationships within your support team—the "one anothers" in your life. It's the doing of life together, not sitting around and explaining it.

As you practice waiting, there is the *action of resting.* Your responsibility is to be anxious for nothing, but to rest in your relationship with Jesus and with others. Now, keep in mind that Jesus may not have direct orders for you today. Don't be in a hurry to the point of being stressed. Following Jesus is all about rest. Jesus calls his disciples into his rest—confident, peaceful, everything-is-going-to-be-OK rest. The action of resting is the act of trusting. In some ways, this is like the athlete who prepares himself for the game, yet knows he must allow the game to come to him rather than pressing to make things happen.

We *are* waiting for Jesus to show up in our lives. We *are* waiting for Jesus to give us answers to our heart's cry—an impression, a peace, a desire, or a thought. We *are* to wait to bring restoration to those God brings us. We *are* to wait for God to bring people into our lives for us to walk with in fellowship and support.

Waiting on Jesus to lead out is demonstrating a ruthless trust in him to come through on our behalf with opportunities and orders for us to follow.

One Day at a Time

Jesus said, "Therefore do not worry about tomorrow, for tomorrow will worry about itself. Each day has enough trouble of its own" (Matthew 6).

I've said it many times:

Yesterday is a cancelled check.

Tomorrow is a promissory note.

Today is the only cash you have.

Alcoholics Anonymous and all of the other Anonymous groups operate upon the theme of "*one day at a time.*" This is exactly what Jesus is saying here—one day at a time. Worry has little to do with the past, but mostly has to do with the future. We worry over what might happen or what might not happen. It's not in our control, but we spend lots of energy as if our worry could make a difference in the outcome. Jesus says "Don't bother!" Each day has plenty of trouble of its own without worrying about tomorrow.

Jesus teaches that if you are seeking his Kingdom and

his righteousness, he will take care of everything else you need. He will do this *one day at a time*. This is what Jesus did with the children of Israel about one month into their 40 years of wandering. He rained down bread from heaven—manna—each day, except on the Sabbath. Each day the manna came down from heaven—each day they were to gather enough for the day, never thinking of storing up some for tomorrow. Each day there was enough.

Jesus is the "new manna in town." Jesus is our daily bread. The word "manna" means a surprise like "what is it?" I see Jesus giving each of us a surprise of his manna, his leadership, his sustenance each and every day for those who seek first his Kingdom and his righteousness. We practice these habits in order to gather the manna for today, which helps in minimizing our worry factor.

Have you noticed that when you think about tomorrow or next week, then the worries become overwhelming? I have to constantly focus my thinking and reflection upon today.

This goes along with the message of the book of Ecclesiastes. King Solomon had tried everything to fill his life with satisfaction and all was found to be empty—luxury, liquor, lust. But at the end of the book he sums up his life's search with two summary truths.

First—Fear God and keep his commandments.

Second—Enjoy your blessings every day.

Paul would say the same thing, but in different terminology. It's all about the simplicity and purity of devotion to Jesus (2 Corinthians 11:3). And that simplicity and purity of devotion is found in these three habits:

- Walking with Jesus.

- Walking with others.

- Waiting on Jesus to lead out with orders and opportunities.

And do all of these . . . *one day at a time.*

CHAPTER 16

What Does It Look Like to Show Off Jesus?

One of my favorite stories of all time is about the VP of Marketing of a dog food company. He stood before his national sales force to give them a rah-rah session.

He moved into gear, "Who has the best dog food in the nation?"

"We do!" they replied.

"Who has the best marketing program in the USA?"

"We do!"

"Who has the best packaging and pricing?"

"We do!"

"Then why is it that out of 19 dog food companies in the country we are number 19?"

No one said a word as everyone fidgeted and squirmed. Then, one brave soul in the back whimpered out an answer: "Because dogs don't like it."

This is the problem we face around the world with the message of Jesus. Jesus has been so enmeshed with Christianity and religiosity that people just don't like it.

I met with a few men who have been studying one of my books, *Mything Out on Jesus and His Teachings*. We discussed my journey following Jesus for nearly four hours over dinner. The response was astounding to me! Listen to this one: "I can truly say that after years of small groups, church, sermons, books, theological treatises, tapes, and lectures, this past engagement with your articulation of the faith is the most personally transforming experience I have had in my own walk. *Jesus!*"

These men, like so many, have been going through the motions of spiritual living, church leadership, and investing in a variety of religious ministries, but they have to hold their noses at times in the process. Without Jesus there isn't anything real to be excited about! We experience this same response wherever we go.

Five Ways of Showing Jesus Off

As followers of Jesus how can we best show Jesus off? How can we best lift Jesus up so people can see him without religious blinders? How can we advance the conversation of Jesus most effectively?

Jesus said that so many are interested, even interested enough to follow (John 4). We're looking for those who are interested. This is really the only requirement that is necessary—to be interested. By the way, if you are interested, you will find all kinds of people interested in the same thing. You will find interested people in churches, mosques, temples, synagogues, civic groups, schools, gyms, in the corporate setting, and in your community. Disciples of Jesus orbit around their world, looking for those who have ears to hear and eyes to see. You're not looking to close any spiritual deals or for people to preach to; you're looking for the interested! They are all around you.

Years ago *The Last Temptation of Christ* movie was released. At best, it was a bad movie and probably would not have lasted more than a couple of weeks in the theaters, but it was actually promoted by Christians. Promoted by Christians? Yes! Christians organized against this movie with signs and angry demonstrations. This drew massive media attention on the demonstrators, which, in turn, attracted more people into the theaters to see the movie.

I learned a great lesson through that experience. Jesus doesn't need or want demonstrations *for* him. Jesus wants his followers to be demonstrations *of* him—do what Jesus would do and say what he would say.

In order to demonstrate Jesus in your world, it's important to be like Jesus in all of your actions. As I've combed through the teachings of Jesus, I have discovered five specific ways to demonstrate him—to show Jesus off!

Lifestyle (Matthew 5)

Jesus says, "You are the light of the world. A city on a hill cannot be hidden. Neither do people light a lamp and put it under a bowl. Instead they put it on its stand, and it gives light to everyone in the house. In the same way, let your light shine before others, that they may see your good deeds and glorify your Father in heaven."

By this we see it is possible for people to be attracted to God through your good deeds—your lifestyle. How you live your life speaks so loudly to those who are watching. How you handle your problems and stresses, how you love your spouse and how you treat your family and friends are all on display. People can see Jesus in this way!

By the way, note there are no words spoken by you here. It's not the fancy or spiritual talk, but the walk that matters most to people. People watch closely for that "ethos"—that credibility in your life. Then, and only then, do your words have any weight. So, show Jesus off with your Jesus lifestyle!

Love One Another (John 13)

Jesus says, "A new command I give you: Love one another. As I have loved you, so you must love one another. By this everyone will know that you are my disciples, if you love one another."

People can also see Jesus by our love for one another. This is so attractive and contagious. People all around you are desperate to love and be loved. Remember what I said earlier: we are not in need of more love in the world, but more lovers.

Jesus is reflected in this kind of love for one another. Jesus is not reflected in the divisiveness of the many religious communities that seem to compete and war against one another. It's ugly and is devoid of the sacrificial love message Jesus came to bring. Jesus prayed that all those who follow him might be one—in unity with him. Jesus unites—all else divides. So, show Jesus off with your love for one another!

Bless When Insulted (I Peter 3)

"Finally, all of you, be like-minded, be sympathetic, love one another, be compassionate and humble. Do not repay evil with evil or insult with insult. On the contrary, repay evil with blessing, because to this you were called so that you may inherit a blessing. For, 'Whoever among you would love life and see good days must keep your tongue from evil and your lips from deceitful speech. Turn from evil and do good; seek peace and pursue it. For the eyes of the Lord are on the righteous and his ears are attentive to their prayer, but the face of the Lord is against those who do evil.' Always be prepared to give an answer to everyone who asks you to give the reason for the hope that you have." People who give a blessing when insulted are acting in a counter-cultural sort of way. It's moving to the beat of a different drummer in the name and spirit of Jesus.

When you bless someone who insults you, people notice you live your life differently from most everyone else who wants to get ahead or who wants to get even. Note that when you act this way, those watching will ask you for the reason for your rare response to the insults sent your way. This is a perfect time to share with those who ask about the Jesus way of life. So, show Jesus off by giving a blessing when you are insulted!

Your Personal Story (Romans 10)

"How, then, can they call on the one they have not believed in? And how can they believe in the one of whom they have not heard? And how can they hear without someone proclaiming it to them?"

This is the only one of the ways we show Jesus off by our words. Note this is not you preaching to or arguing with anyone. The best thing to share is your own personal story. No one can argue with your own experience, strength, and hope you have found through knowing and following Jesus. This book is an example of sharing my personal journey of Jesus apprehending me. Don't be afraid to share your story. When you are a follower of Jesus, your story is really Jesus' story through you!

Jesus sent out his early followers without giving them a set speech or presentation. He took an entirely different approach. He promised them that they would be given what to say by his Spirit. So, quit talking so much and start embracing Jesus as a lifestyle, learn how to love one another, then he will give you what to say when you need it.

Ministering to the Needy (Matthew 25)

Jesus says something very unique, "For I was hungry and you gave me something to eat; I was thirsty and you gave me something to drink; I was a stranger and you invited me in; naked and you clothed me; I was sick and you visited me; I was in prison, and you came to me.' Then the righteous will answer him, 'Lord, when did we see you hungry and feed you, or thirsty and give you something to drink? And when did we see you a stranger and invite you in, or naked and clothe you? When did we see you sick or in prison and come to you?' The King will answer and say to them, 'Truly I say to you, to the extent that you did it to one of these brothers of mine, even the least of them, you did it to me.'"

Once a month a group of us feed and minister to the needs of the homeless in Orange County. I always encourage each of the volunteers that by loving and ministering to these dear people they are actually ministering to Jesus himself.

Jesus reveals another way that will have a most definite impact in the world and demonstrates the heart of Jesus. Here the sacrificial love message of Jesus is spread by being aware of Jesus' heart and that Jesus can be found in those in need in our world—the hungry, the thirsty, the naked, the stranger, the sick, and those in prison.

Jesus also spoke directly to those who didn't notice Jesus in the midst of the needy. "He will reply, 'Truly I tell you, whatever you did not do for one of the least of these, you did not do for me.' When we are aware of the poor and needy around us, we are demonstrating the heart of Jesus in our world. Jesus always sought them out and so should we. And when we do, the attractiveness of the sacrificial love of Jesus shines through. Again, there is no talking required here.

Now, each of these actions shows Jesus off to the world—*living a lifestyle like Jesus, loving one another, blessing when insulted, sharing your own story, and helping those in need*. In fact, when you do these things, you are living a lifestyle on a different level altogether and people notice. The people who notice are all of the people who are watching you day after day. This is Kingdom living at its core!

Every morning when I wake up, I say something to Jesus. I say, "good morning, Jesus! What do you have for me to do today?" With this greeting and question I set out on a most amazing adventure—every day! Like everyone else, I have all kinds of appointments throughout my day. However, I am looking to see where Jesus might show up, whether in a scheduled appointment, (where I know who I'm meeting and when it is), a spontaneous appointment (where I know the person, but hadn't planned on seeing him today), or a surprise appointment (where I don't know the person and had no idea I might meet him).

Just today, I was writing this chapter in a local restaurant, when I had a spontaneous appointment with an old friend and his wife. They don't live here. I haven't seen them for more than 20 years. We noticed one another at the same time and instantly embraced. They were such an encouragement to me as he expressed their love for me and reminded me twice that we are friends. Then, as I left the restaurant later, my friend walked me outside and said, "I believe this was an appointment set up by God for us to run into one another." There was no doubt in my mind!

I believe God is setting up divine appointments all day long just for you. He wants to love and touch people through you. He sets these appointments up! All He wants from you is for you to show up! Show up and you'll be showing Jesus off at the same time.

By the way, most of the time Jesus' divine appointments he has for you will seem like interruptions in your schedule—even irritations. When an interruption or irritation arises, look for what Jesus might be up to! Jesus delights in doing amazing things in his way and in his time.

CHAPTER 17

What Is Your End Game?

After many discussions with my wife and after many hours of thinking about it, we struggled with putting this chapter first. If there is a significant takeaway from this book, we believe this chapter is it.

We recently attended a special 9/11 event at Mariners Church in southern California, where the Muslim-Christian divide was addressed by several speakers and a series of table discussions.

At our first table discussion one of the Pastors from Mariners asked, "Tim, what would you say to Christians about relating to Muslims?"

I answered him with, "I believe Christians have the wrong end game as they approach Muslims. Christians have the end game of luring, persuading, and even converting Muslims in order to make them Christians. Making Muslims Christians only deepens the great division between them." I continued, "Why would you *want* to make a Muslim a Christian?"

I've engaged in this conversation on lots of occasions. The usual response to me is the thoughtful nodding of the head, then silence.

Last year in Bethlehem, we caught up with one of the superstars of Christianity, who was speaking at a Palestinian Christian conference. This teacher was the first to ever share with me how easy it was to teach the Bible in the Muslim mosques around the world. Then, he asked, "What are you doing now?" I told him we are doing our best to follow Jesus personally and to introduce Jesus into the many cultures of the world. He quickly replied, "Yes, we must do our best to bring them into Christianity." He was on his way to Gaza to spend time with his Muslim friends with the end game of somehow, someway, someday making them Christians. Instead of arguing with a much older Christian icon, I kept reframing his words to mean introducing them to Jesus.

Several years ago, a friend of mine was visiting people in northern India. By that time, my friend had really learned what it means to live out the principles of Jesus—to avoid any and all conversion tactics and to focus on advancing the conversation of Jesus. He made a new friend in India who was a missionary to the Hindus. The mission work was not going well, unless his goal was to suffer persecution, death threats, and cultural oppression.

He introduced his new friend to our daily podcast/blog, "Jesus Plus Nothing." Between my friend and me, our missionary "got it" right away. He quickly understood why he was suffering so much with very few finding Jesus. His end game was all about converting Hindus into Christians. When he changed his approach, his work among the Hindus became more effective. You see, before, he had the wrong end game, and it didn't work!

Church leaders are becoming more and more concerned over why so many churches are shutting down in the U.S. today. For the most part, churches aren't experiencing genuine new growth. Instead, most mega-churches grow through transference—people transferring from other churches that have shut down or transferring from other churches that couldn't meet their consumer needs. Honest leaders know this is true, therefore they look for new ways to reach out to new "prospects."

A pastor of one of the local mega-churches asked me to advise him on how to reach out to the many ethnic cultures in the area. I asked him two questions: one, "Is your goal to bring them into your church?" Two, "Is your goal to make them Christians?" He answered, "Yes!" to both.

If coming to church or becoming a Christian is your end game, you will most certainly turn the people you want to attract away from you.

At the last President's National Prayer Breakfast I had the privilege of speaking at one of the regional dinners. "What's Your End Game?" was my topic. Afterward, a Pakistani introduced himself to me. He said, "I am a Christian who plants churches in Pakistan." Shocked, I said, "Really! How is that working for you?" He said, "Not well. We are threatened and persecuted continually! We fear for our lives and for the lives of those who convert to Christianity." Tragically, his Christian Cabinet Member friend who was standing with him as we talked was assassinated three weeks later upon his return to Pakistan.

He continued, "Through your talk tonight, I see we have the wrong end game. We need to introduce Pakistanis to Jesus and stop trying to convert them to Christianity." That was the most satisfying experience after speaking that I've had in years! This pastor not only listened; he really did "get it."

Or did he?

I asked, "What are you going to do to change your approach?" He said, "I want to spend some time with you before I return to Pakistan." "That's a good idea!" I chimed in.

When I shared this story with my good friend, Scott, he said, "So, now he's made a *second* mistake in choosing his end game! First, your Pakistani friend mistakenly made Christianity his end game; then he mistakenly made *you* his end game." Sadly, I was so enthused about moving my friend off Christianity as an end game that I didn't mind him making me his new end game. If you are not careful, your mission for Jesus can easily compete with Jesus' mission.

This demonstrates clearly and painfully how easy it is to talk a good game about Jesus without embracing Jesus for yourself. This is why writing this book has become a passion for us.

Please listen carefully to this statement: *Unless Jesus is your end game, then your life amounts to nothing. Jesus said it himself: "Without me you can do nothing"* (John 15). The Apostle Paul also agreed, saying that his entire life and his accomplishments were a pile of manure compared to knowing Jesus. Without Jesus as *your* end game, your life will be filled with frustrations in your religious experience. You will have disappointments with life's expectations, anxiety over whether your children will follow in your religious traditions, concern over the lifestyle decisions of your children and grandchildren, fears for your future security, terror over immediate financial concerns, and discouragement with life's results.

These are not just theoretical experiences, but they have been our experiences without Jesus as *our* end game! Now that Jesus is our life's end game, all of these worries and concerns take on a different perspective altogether. We have found Jesus, simply Jesus, more than adequate in every way. This is not a religious experience, but a personal one.

Making Jesus your end game initiates the process of stripping away all add-ons to Jesus and totally devoting your life, loved ones, and livelihood to Jesus plus nothing else. To make Christ your end game will not work! Jesus warned us, "There are many Christs" (Matthew 24). To make your religion your end game will not work! There are many religions! To make your church your end game will not work! To make your religious traditions your end game will not work! Jesus—the name above all names and the person above all persons—is the only possible end game that matters. You may say this is just semantics, but it isn't. This is personal. His name is Jesus!

Jesus made it very clear in his teachings that he is the only end game necessary.

Jesus said to the religious leaders, "You study the

Scriptures diligently because you think that in them you possess eternal life. These are the very Scriptures that testify about *me*, yet you refuse to come to *me* to have life" (John 5:39-40). Jesus was not their end game; the Scriptures were!

In addition to Jesus saying, "Without *me* you can do nothing," Jesus emphasized how vital it is for his followers to hang on to him in the same way a branch must remain attached to the vine. He said, "Abide in *me*" (John 15).

In the first few pages of this book, we examined the first breakfast meeting Jesus had with his disciples after the resurrection at the shores of Galilee. Jesus made it very clear that all he really cared about was their personal relationship with him by asking, "Do you love *me*?" three times. Jesus' intention was to make himself the end game for every follower.

Immediately after this encounter, an intriguing conversation occurs with Peter. Jesus said to Peter, "When you were younger you dressed yourself and went where you wanted; but when you are old you will stretch out your hands, and someone else will dress you and lead you where you do not want to go." Jesus said this to indicate the kind of death by which Peter would die. Then Jesus said to him, "Follow *me*!"

It's important to note what happens next. Peter turned and saw that John was following them. When Peter saw him, he asked, "Lord, what about him?" Jesus answered, "If I want him to remain alive until I return, what is that to you? You must follow *me*" (John 21:5-23). In other words, it's none of your business how Jesus relates to anyone else. Make it your business to relate to Jesus personally—*make Jesus your end game.*

At one of Jesus' final meetings with his disciples, he gave them a mandate. Jesus said, "All authority in heaven and on earth has been given to *me*. Therefore go and make disciples of all nations" (Matthew 28:19-20). Followers of

Jesus are not to make disciples of their religious persuasion. They are not to make disciples of local religious affiliation. They are not to make disciples of their culture. They are to make disciples of Jesus!

Before Jesus' ascension into heaven, he directed his disciples to wait in Jerusalem. Jesus said, "But you will receive power when the Holy Spirit comes on you; and you will be *my* witnesses in Jerusalem, and in all Judea and Samaria, and to the ends of the earth" (Acts 1:8). They are not to bear witness of their particular religious persuasion. They were not to bear witness about their local religious affiliation. They are not to bear witness about their cultural distinctives. They are to bear witness of Jesus throughout the world!

When your stress, troubles, cultural, and religious struggles overwhelm you, remember Jesus' invitation, "Come to *me*, all you who are weary and burdened, and I will give you rest. Take my yoke upon you and learn from *me*, for I am gentle and humble in heart, and you will find rest for your souls. For my yoke is easy and my burden is light" (John 11:28-30).

Jesus said, "I am the good shepherd; I know my sheep and my sheep know *me*. . . . I have other sheep that are not of this sheep pen. I must bring them also. They too will listen to *my* voice, and there shall be one flock and one shepherd" (John 10:14-16). You can get the guidance you really need from Jesus, the shepherd? This guidance can only be found in your day-to-day, relationship with Jesus. You can get to know him and know what he wants by talking with him daily and often. Sometimes, we would rather have a good scripture verse or rule to follow. At times this seems easier, but Jesus doesn't want it this way. He wants you to stop and listen. Why would Jesus say you can listen to his voice, if it weren't true? Are you listening to his voice?

So, how do you hear the voice of Jesus? We have found and want to offer five basics to prepare you for hearing the voice of Jesus:

First—Immerse yourself in the Scriptures. Read, reread and meditate on the Scriptures as you would a love letter, not a research paper. Always search for Jesus wherever you are reading, not getting sidetracked with anything else. Remember it's the spirit of the law, not the letter of the law. This was the mistake the religious leaders who confronted Jesus made and he was continually correcting them. They were so wrapped up in Bible memory and organizing the Scriptures into doctrinal systems that they missed Jesus in the process. Jesus can be seen throughout these Scriptures.

It is fascinating to me to think about what Scriptures existed, when Jesus was working with his disciples. It was the Law or Torah, the Writings, which included the Proverbs and the Psalms and then the Prophets. When Jesus was confronted and tempted by the devil in the wilderness, Jesus quoted Scripture to resist the evil one. He quoted verses out of Deuteronomy. Then we see Jesus walking with two disciples on the road to Emmaus. In Luke 24:27 it is recorded: He said to them, "This is what I told you while I was still with you: Everything must be fulfilled that is written about me in the Law of Moses, the Prophets and the Psalms." Then he opened their minds so they could understand the Scriptures. Jesus walked them through the Law, the Prophets and the Psalms in order to open their minds about himself.

Then Philip had a very special divine appointment with the Ethiopian eunuch who was reading the scroll of Isaiah in his chariot. In Acts 8:35 it says: Then Philip began with that very passage of Scripture and told him the good news about Jesus. Philip used the prophet Isaiah's writings to teach this interested official about Jesus.

Second—Be aware of the Jesus themes throughout the Scriptures. In order to seek Jesus in the Scriptures, especially the Law, the Prophets, and the Psalms, look for the major themes about Jesus. For instance, there is the theme of the glory or the Shekinah glory—the visible presence of God—throughout. Beginning with the presence of God in the Garden, the burning bush, the pillar of fire by night and the cloud by day that led the children of Israel through the wilderness, the star of Bethlehem and then Jesus is the ultimate Shekinah glory—the visible presence of God—on earth. Note how many times the Angel of the Lord or the Angel of Jehovah appeared in the Old Testament. Most think this was actually Jesus. Jesus was the uniquely born one—the holy one of Israel—born of a virgin by the Spirit of God. Muslims refer to Jesus as the son of Mary, Spirit of God, and the Messiah. To them Jesus or Isa is the "ruhallah"—from the Spirit of God.

Jesus fulfilled and gave meaning to every mark and letter of the Mosaic Law. Jesus fulfilled every longing of the heart of the Psalms. And, Jesus also fulfilled the many Messianic prophecies. These prophecies seem to speak of Jesus and find their culmination in him, so look for those themes that find their way to Jesus.

Third—Count on his wisdom. If you are seeking to hear and listen to the voice of Jesus, ask for his wisdom as you live your life the best you can. In one of the early writings of the New Covenant—the book of James—there is a very insightful passage: If any of you lacks wisdom, you should ask God, who gives generously to all without finding fault, and it will be given to you. But when you ask, you must believe and not doubt, because the one who doubts is like a wave of the sea, blown and tossed by the wind. Those who doubt should not think they will receive anything from the Lord; they are double-minded and unstable in all they do (James 1). I ask for wisdom every day and sometimes many times a day and I count on it as I make decisions, wanting to hear the voice of Jesus as I move through the day.

Fourth—Be sure to seek Jesus within the context of a few. One of the most important ways for you to hear the voice of Jesus is to operate within a supportive community. It's learning to "hear and practice" his words together. Remember, it's when two or three are gathered together in the name of Jesus that Jesus will show up and make his presence known. When this happens, you will recognize and hear his voice through another.

Fifth—Discipline yourself to listen when you pray. When you pray, don't just do all of the talking and asking; take the time to listen for an answer. This seems so simple, yet it is very difficult to do. It takes some painful discipline to sit quietly and listen. You will find these five basics to be most helpful as you seek to hear the voice of Jesus in times like these.

There is one more thing in hearing and listening for the voice of Jesus. It may be the most critical dimension of all! In John 6, Jesus was asked: "What must we do to do the work of God?" Jesus answers this most simply with: "The work of God is this: *trust the one God has sent.*" Or, simply put: learn to trust Jesus with everything—your security, your family, your business, your future—everything! When you have the courage to trust Jesus with everything, believe me, you will hear and listen to what he has to say. This is the ultimate expression Jesus is looking for as you learn to respond to his most revolutionary words ever: *Follow me!*

I think Jesus is saying to each of us: "Can you hear me now?

When you are overwhelmed with troubles and trials, ask Jesus about it. He's been there, done that! When you can't stand the pain any longer, ask Jesus. He's been there, done that! When you feel betrayed, rejected, and discounted, ask Jesus. He's been there, done that! When you just lost your loved one by death, ask Jesus. He's been there, done that! When God seems to be late coming through for you, ask Jesus about it.

If you want to make Jesus your end game, your best action step is to take whatever is on your mind and heart to Jesus first. When I find myself talking more to people about my problems than I do Jesus, then I know Jesus isn't my end game.

Today, Jesus of Nazareth still stands at the highest pinnacle of all humanity. There are over 147 million items in the Library of Congress, extending to over 838 miles of bookshelves and more are about Jesus than any other person who ever lived.

Jesus is a great man, yet he is more than just a great man. His life and lifestyle speak more loudly than his teachings. When it comes to making sense out of life, all you have to do is ask the question, "What would Jesus do?" and you already have your answer! This is a universal question that anyone (Christian, Muslim, Jew, Buddhist, Hindu, non-religious) can ask and be helped by the answer. Jesus is the only one who can be said to be the lifestyle of the universe! The lifestyle of the universe is not a code; it's a character. His name is Jesus. Jesus has become a universal reference point for moral behavior for many.

Jesus is the most quoted teacher ever, yet he is more than a teacher. You would be hard-pressed to find any self-help principles taught today that do not find their origin in the teachings of Jesus. His wisdom and insights rank higher than any spiritual guru. In fact, several of the most recent gurus used Jesus as their source . . . without giving him any credit.

Jesus is the most unique prophet, yet he is more than a prophet. I'm fascinated that one of the best known of the Hindu culture, Mahatma Gandhi, purposely followed the teachings and example of Jesus. Gandhi was so adored by his people that he was called Christ-like. I'm amazed that the best-known Buddhist, His Holiness the 14th Dalai Lama, Tenzin Gyatso, said that he is unworthy of tying the shoes of Jesus.

It's well known that the Holy Bible treats Jesus as a great prophet, but few know that the Holy Qur'an presents him as the only supernatural prophet. Even Jewish scholars have begun to recognize Jesus as the most popular rabbi ever. Agnostics and atheists have lots of trouble with religion, but not with Jesus. I know Muslims, Jews, Buddhists, Hindus, Christians, atheists and agnostics who follow Jesus and view him as more than a Prophet.

Jesus is more than a great man, more than a good teacher or guru, more than a credible brand, and more than a prophet. These are proper labels for Jesus and all true. However, these labels don't necessarily make a difference in a person's life . . . *until* you make Jesus your end game.

Thank you for following me on this journey of words. I hope it encourages you to follow the one who is the Word. Who is the way. The truth. The life.

I can't say the journey will be easy.

I *can* say you will never regret it.

As a postscript to what I have written, I wanted to share with you a quote I came across just a few weeks before I submitted this manuscript to the publisher. It is a quote by Albert Schweitzer. If you are not familiar with him, or only vaguely familiar, he was an extraordinary man.

He had three doctorates. In philosophy, theology, and medicine. He was also a well-respected author. On top of that, he was a concert organist and a world authority on Bach. Yet he left that ivory-towered world with its promises of fame and fortune, and he buried himself in the dark and dangerous jungles of Africa for a sweltering life of service to the poor and needy.

Why?

Because he was a follower of Jesus. And Africa is where Jesus led him. Although some of his theological beliefs were unorthodox, his devotion to Jesus was one of unswerving obedience. He read the story of the rich man and Lazarus in the Bible and realized that Europe was the rich man and Africa was Lazarus. He felt compassion for the plight of the people there, and he decided that once he finished his medical degree he would dedicate the rest of his life to serving them. He touched them and healed them, much the way Jesus did when he walked the earth. He fed them, gathered them together, much the way Jesus did. And he did this for almost 60 years until the day he died. He was dedicated to serving humanity in the name of Jesus and had a clear understanding of the Kingdom of

God. He wrote something similar to what I have said about the inwardness we must cultivate if we are ever to live a Kingdom lifestyle.

In his *Memoirs of Childhood and Youth,* he writes:

> The miracle must happen in us before it can happen in the world. We dare not set our hope on our own efforts to create the conditions for God's Kingdom in the world. We must indeed labor for its realization. But there can be no Kingdom of God in the world without the Kingdom of God in our hearts. The starting point is our determined effort to bring every thought and action under the sway of the Kingdom of God. Nothing can be achieved without inwardness. The Spirit of God will only strive against the spirit of the world when it has won its victory over that spirit in our hearts.

Then there's the quote I mentioned earlier, the one I came across a few weeks before this book went to the publisher. I can't stop thinking about it.

> Jesus comes to us as One unknown, without a name, as of old, by the lake-side. He came to those men who knew Him not. He speaks to us the same word: "Follow me!" and sets us to the tasks, which He has to fulfill for our time. He commands. And to those who obey Him, whether they be wise or simple. He will reveal Himself in the toils, the conflicts, the sufferings, which they shall pass through in His fellowship, and, as an ineffable mystery, they shall learn in their own experience Who He is.

There is a part of Jesus we can't know by reading books about him, can't know by listening to sermons on him.

There is a part of him we can't know by going to church, to Bible college, to seminary. There is a part of him we can only know by following him. The way Peter followed him. And James. And John. And the rest of the original 12.

As they walked with him, they watched him and worked with him. He showed them things he never showed to the masses, shared with them things he never shared with the crowds. He answered their questions. He spoke into their lives. He loved them. Taught them. Washed their feet. He did, as Schweitzer said, reveal himself in the toils, the conflicts, and the sufferings, which they passed through in his fellowship. And, as he said, they learned in their own unique experience who Jesus is.

Jesus plus nothing.

An incredible offer is extended to you with the words, "Follow me."

Come with us, won't you, and follow him.

Come and be challenged.

Come and be changed.

The world will be a better place if you do.

Your world will be a better place if you do.

There's an old story that I told once a year for 22 years as a pastor. If you haven't heard it, you will love it. If you have heard it, be reminded and apply it.

Four people boarded a small airplane—the pilot, a priest, a Boy Scout and a computer executive. On their way to their destination it became obvious the plane was in trouble. The pilot emerged out of the cockpit and said, "This plane is going down! There are four of us onboard, but we only have three parachutes. I have a young wife and three children. I can't leave them alone, so I'm taking one of these parachutes and jumping." The pilot jumped!

The computer executive stood up and said, "I was just named 'the smartest man in all of the world' in a major business magazine. If I were to go down with this plane, the world would take such a loss. I'm taking one of these parachutes and jumping." The computer executive jumped!

As the Priest sized up the situation, he knew what he had to do. He said, "My son, I am old and ready to meet my Maker. You are young with a full life ahead of you. You take that last parachute and save yourself." He said this with deep emotion, beginning to weep.

The Boy Scout put his arm around the Priest and said, "Calm down, Father, the smartest man in all the world just grabbed my knapsack and jumped out of the plane."

This is a picture of life. At some point in your life, you are going to have to make that fatal jump. It doesn't matter how smart you are. What matters most is: "Do you have a parachute?"

Jesus is the only parachute you'll ever need.

Try reframing your end game into JESUS...plus... nothing.

FOR MORE ON "JESUS PLUS NOTHING"

WEBSITES:

www.jesusplusnothing.org <http://www.jesusplusnothing.org>

www.timtimmons.com <http://www.timtimmons.com>

AUDIOBOOK

SUBSCRIBE TO DAILY PODCAST/BLOG: "JESUS PLUS NOTHING DAILY"

LIBRARY OF AUDIO, VIDEO SERIES

FACEBOOK: www.facebook.com/jesusplusnothing <http://www.facebook.com/jesusplusnothing>

TWITTER: ttimmonssr

JESUS PLUS NOTHING Curriculum

(To be released soon!)